LEXICON of AWESOME

Absolutely Unprofessional
Wadsworth, OH

First edition diligently edited by Britt Clarke at brittclarke.com

Cover art by R. J Dyson. Cover and interior layout and design by Absolutely Unprofessional.

Definitions sourced and adapted from Merriam-Webster.com

First Printing: 2020
Second Edition: 2023
ISBN 979-8-9879116-3-1
Absolutely Unprofessional
rjdysonsblog.com
absolutelyunprofessional.com

The Lexicon

To Brooke. My favorite traveling mate.

Divine words, written and spoken, unlock a better way. And Word in the flesh reveals it to us.

A

Aha!

Awesome[1] is one of those incredible words that gets thrown around without its full weight coming to bear. When my little Ada flips on the jungle gym at the school playground, I'll throw out an "Awesome!" like a reflex. I mean it too. It's super fun to watch her take chances and challenges and own them one flip at a time. I find myself genuinely impressed at the progression of ability in those little arms and bones, heart and flesh. Her spirit glows with success, lighting up my day in tandem.

These are those lowercase-A awesome moments in life. Personally captivating. But as reflexes go, I'm also quick to toss out a breathy "That...was...awesome!" when my son hits a slippery patch on the floor between the dining room and the living room and biffs it without warning. Tousled hair. Knees bent in ways that turn the stomach. Is it really awesome? Is it really something to be impressed by? Something that stirs a genuine sense of wonder and awe in the power at hand?

Not really. It's a careless word spit. These moments can be astounding, but they're not necessarily awesome.

Terror, on the other hand, is found at the heart of something awesome. Something so mighty and powerful and wonder-stirring that I'm temporarily paralyzed, frozen to the gully. Other times in the face of awesomeness I helplessly drop facedown in worship.

The birth of a child.

The death of a spouse.

Victory in battle.

Witnessing atrocity.

The realization of a dream.

I remember the first summer I read about Jesus' feeding at least five thousand people with a couple fish and a handful of bread loaves. I can still feel that knot in my chest. Something deep inside unsettled by that power and mystery—something so curious, experienced by so many people, told and retold, written and rewritten by kids and their parents and their neighbors and disciples. I was shaken by the awesomeness of Christ two thousand years after He mysteriously broke some fish and bread, terrified and excited at the same time. That was capital-A awesome. This is that divine type of awesome that surpasses all other awesomes.

How is it that such a profound feeling can be whipped up by words in sentences on a page from an ancient journal?

Words carry divine weight, don't they?

When was the last time something genuinely, terrifyingly, extraordinarily awesome took your breath away? Something wildly powerful and mysterious spoken in your presence that captivated your mind and whisked you away to a divine time and space.

My son wiping out on the floor? Crazy funny. My daughter growing and inspiring? Deeply moving. God's slow and steady work through suffering and success? Awesome.

/ / /

Then there's a word like **advent**[2], the arrival of a noteworthy person or thing.

The beginning of an awesome adventure.

The intense birth of my Joanna in a sea of hospital staff.

Brooke walking down that aisle in the grass under a radiant sun.

The first coffee with a dude on his new journey with Creator God in hope and passion and truth.

Six-year-old Ada stepping from the platform beneath a zip line into thin air.

My dude Elias bombing a small hill on his longboard for the first time.

Discovering that thing, at age thirty-seven, which the Creator designed me to devote my journey to while in this body, on this patch of dirt, with these talents and skills and desires and offerings.

The coming of Creator-Savior in the flesh. The Advent of all advents.

Our homes are fertile ground for these advents. Moments that often take us by surprise, don't they? The hair on the back of our necks stand tall at the prospect of a new venture, or we may drop to our knees as though we've ruptured an aorta in a jarring moment of crystal clarity and curiosity. Loaded with divine power and depth of insight, advents connect our spirit and our flesh and our imagination on a soul-deep level between the walls of our homes.

Aha[3] moments change us. Like when I realized my marriage was bigger and better thirteen years in. They're pivotal and comforting, like God journeying alongside His people, thick and thin, day after year after millennium. "Be courageous," Moses said. "The Lord your

God travels with you, and He will never leave you and never abandon you."[4] Realizing that Christ's thick and thin will always be thicker than my thinnest attitude is unexplainably relieving. And that my life with Brooke is thicker and fuller the longer we travel side by side, covered in the dust of the Teacher? Awesome.

But aha moments also appear in small and peculiar ways, like discovering the perfect charcoal spread beneath the tenderloin, beautifully arrayed below the grate, glowing and breathing like the belly of a dragon in a drafty cave. Some aha moments are flat-out delicious.

/ / /

And of course there's **Ada**[5], an amazing A full of life and silliness, a beautiful addition to the Dyson brood. Before Ada was born, before she was even a thought, she was the vision of a toddler holding my hand on the beach with a dropping sun behind gentle waves washing our feet.

Ada means "precious ornament" or "beautiful addition." She is. And she's filled to the brim with aha moments at home and on the monkey bars, with crayons and thicker and thicker chapter books, on hikes and with food.

One morning, as we were sharing a booth at Panera, eating bagels with a small cup of water and a hot coffee between us, she grasped at the concept of light. We were reading about the time Jesus challenged His people to let their light shine, in crowds and on hills and in basements, classrooms and factories. "Don't cover the light, don't hide it," He said. "A light is useless smothered and covered. Let your light shine. Let everyone see the good life you're living and worship Me because of it."[6]

Ada was drawing a picture in her journal of a light on a hill, and next to it stood a bunch of stick people with smiles—really big, funky smiles—

and wild, bright clothes.

"Ada, who are the people around the light on the hill?"

"Well, when we let our light shine, it brightens everyone's day."

/ / /

Aha moments happen in pits, on mountaintops, and over coffee and barbeque. They happen when our hearts and minds are open just enough for the light to stream in. To be honest, the default position of my attitude is pretty bleak. Can you imagine how many surprise discoveries I've missed with my face in the mud, behind locked doors, covered in past grit? It's a depressing thought. Yet, hope for what might be is infinitely more powerful.

"Aha!" We've all done it. We've literally shouted, "Yikes!" or "Great Scott!" or "Fart nuggets!" I'm not ashamed to say I've screeched a fantastical, "Aha! I can't believe I didn't think of that before!" Of course, had I thought of it before I wouldn't have shouted "Aha!"

There are a lot of ways to engage these electrifying moments. Some are the overflow of a joy-filled discovery. Some are only found in the bathroom stall of a gutter pub.

"Oh, God!" Then I crawl out of the ditch and go home to my family.

"I get it now!" as I watch my son step forward, away from the wall of indecision, pulled into the orbit of carpe diem.

"Goodnight! I can't spend another day like this," when it hits that I've bought into those festering, self-deprecating lies again.

These God-breathed discoveries pump waves of blood through each limb as we stumble through that next step, propelled into the future.

These awesome experiences are necessary for growth. Not simply our own, but the growth of our kids watching us crawl, walk, and then stand firm. I'm not sure if these happen every day or not, but we tend to recognize the feel and the sound of God when they do.

How do you prepare your heart and mind and soul to experience an awesome aha moment?

How are you preparing your kids' for these awesome aha moments?

I know, I know, we don't *plan* these moments, right? No, I guess not. But we can plan on them. We can live with our eyes, ears, and hearts open. We can engage life with the attitude of a new creation, even imperfectly, and step into the advent of a new day. I've found that reading the Word with a humble mind and a willing spirit at sunrise opens my eyes. Of course, we can't make the aha appear from within the magic lamp, but we can set the stage for it.

I'm convinced that a hundred little ahas can make a dent in an otherwise dreary Ohio dream.

B

Bandera of Dreams

Have you ever had to hold up a dream for someone? Nail it to a pole and wave it back and forth so they can see it clear and alive, far above the fray?

When my kids were learning to walk, each in their own season, this was our job. Brooke and I sat them down on the floor, stable and strong, then we'd jog to the other side of the room and begin to wave, shouting, "Come on, make your move, you can totally do this!"

After all, new adventures have to begin somewhere. Like each of my kids learning to crawl before standing upright. Then, before we knew it, they took ownership of the goal, the dream to walk and we no longer waved that bandera so high.

You've never heard of the bandera of dreams? **Bandera**[1] is Spanish for "flag" or "banner." More loosely, it's the various colors on a flag that represent an idea, that serve as a symbol. The bandera of dreams does just that. For my kids shuffling around on their knees all day long, that bandera symbolized walking. Of course, it was also my dream for them, so I waved it high, fully aware of the freedom they would have if they chased after it.

I get to carry close friends' banderas too. Yeah, you know what I mean.

I raise their bandera to the sky when they're motivated to leap from the platform. I hold it steady as they soar far above the dream-eating culture zombies, onward into their unfolding future. I wave it like a shimmering beacon that cuts through the fog to guide their squinting eyes and stumbling feet.

Christ does this. It's part of what draws me to Him. "I am the way to absolute rescue. I am the truth of it all. I am the real life."[2] Christ is The Bandera of all Banderas. Raised high, He's the symbol of sacrificial love when I'm broken. Raised from the tomb, He's new life when I'm ready for the grave. But He's more than a banner and a symbol. Christ is an endlessly divine mystery inviting us into His reality through a lifetime of aha moments. He invites us to wake up another day, raise the flag and conquer the next hill.

/ / /

Beginnings are like births. Now that's a good word, **birth**[3]. There's so much imagery and symbolism and life packed into it. Birth is exciting. Birth is Christmas. It's an emergence of new life and breath. It's the advent of a fresh hope and a bright future.

Brooke[4], the incredible woman who birthed our three children, the one who carried the brunt, to put it mildly, of the awesome struggle involved in growing, caring for and birthing multiple children in multiple seasons of life—she understands the blessing of new birth and new life in a way that I can't. I'm a dude. A husband. I spent my time supporting Brooke from a safe distance once that significant act of conception moved beyond the concept of a wonderful act. Click-click. Wink-wink.

I don't pretend to understand the full-scale, messy-divine process unfolding in a womb, but I felt it in my soul with the advent of every child.

Have you seen images of a baby in process in the womb? I mean, really looked at them? The spinal cord and the lungs and those tiny little digits wiggling like inchworms on a branch. Advent. I've stared at these candid baby photos. They change things. They turn the soul like garden soil. Divine life just beneath the surface, ready to sprout.

But it isn't just the images that catch me off guard during those nine or so months, it's also the stark reality of a new life soon to be entirely dependent on me and my wife and our capacity to love and sacrifice. I hear it's like adoption, that wildly exciting journey from a hope and a dream to the possibility on through the reality of a living and breathing child under the roof of your home. A messy process felt around every turn.

The birth of a new adventure.

/ / /

For years I've held on to a passion for writing. I feel alive when I write. When a story winds its way up from my gut on through the mind and into the page, everything else disappears. So that's it, right? Passion discovered, passion pursued, passion realized? Hardly.

I've also had this floating dream of owning a bookstore in a small but growing tourist trap town. Brooke and I both let this one creep in from time to time. It's unrealistic, undeveloped, impractical and every other *un* and *im* in the English language, but it's also exciting and unifying. Did I mention that a bed and breakfast would be a sweet endeavor too?

Dreams and ideas and passions and skills and talents and desires jam and wither in a **bottleneck**[5] of floundering possibilities and undeveloped vision. Bottlenecks impede flow. Sometimes it's by design, like to keep wine from gushing out when pouring. Other times bottlenecks are simply poor planning, clogging the works.

When a dozen opportunities arise, the bandera of dreams is held firm, an intentional bottleneck for clarity and focus. Or when a dozen obstacles gunk up the works, the bandera draws us forward in an orderly fashion. Step by step. Breath by breath. Hazard by hope. My kids magnify these bottlenecks too. With the messy advent of each child Brooke and I seem to be constantly raising new banderas high. One bandera after another. So many dreams it can be hard to find my own in the mix. Some days we flail around like air dancers at a used car lot, grasping for anything and everything. Some days move like a graceful slow dance of intertwining dreams, goals, and actions. Yet this is the merciful blessing of a bottleneck, isn't it? As a family, we're forced to slow down together, catch a fresh glimpse of God's desire, wave our banderas in unison, then climb the day's hill on purpose.

Yeah, writing stirs a fresh wind, but that wind only stirs my passion when it complements my role as a dad climbing hills shoulder to shoulder with my kids. And when it bottlenecks? Well, I'm surrounded by a tribe more than willing to take a step back, tussle the banners and move set out on mission together again.

There's power in being a bandera-bearer. In holding up our own, for sure, but lifting up the hopes and dreams of those closest to us? Awesome.

/ / /

I don't know about you, but I want to know that my short time in the flesh is well spent along the trail in tents, not caves. I want to journey with a vision that moves and climbs, not hobble around with an emaciated attitude gasping for breath. And who knows, maybe I'll own a bed and breakfast in a van down by the river someday too.

So this begs the question, what bandera of dreams are you holding high? Picture life five years from now. What do you see on the horizon?

Whether you've connected the dots to your dream or have buried it six feet under, are you weaving and hoisting a new bandera for a new season?

Every morning I rise, brew some Breakfast Blend and spend time in the ancient Text of that way, truth and life. I have yet to find a better perch from which to view my bandera. And I pray. Imagine, I get to lift up my vision to the Creator of Vision, release it into His care on a daily basis and patiently anticipate movement.

Of course, there's no guarantee that my current bandera will manifest as I imagine it, but that's not the point. These rising and falling banderas release me free from my own stunted and stalled initiatives. They draw me forward, stir my mind to action and foster a hope beyond the bandera itself. A divine hope sourced in the only God who can understand my stifled, "Lord, I don't know where I'm headed, but, dear God, would you show me a better way?"

Several years ago, I distilled my personal movement into a one-sentence vision, a mountaintop view of how I'd love to see God mature and use me here in the dirt. No doubt it'll be rewritten and refined as I discover more and more about the Creator and who I am here and now through unforeseen aha moments sprouting in the distance. But that's part of the journey isn't it? The ongoing mysterious tension of what is and what could be.

Which begs the question, what about you? What about your bandera? Sometimes it helps to sketch out a picture of what could be. Spend some time in prayer and then journal, paint or write a song about what transpires. Keep it close to your chest for a season continually leaning into the Vision-maker as you give birth to your pursuit.

C

Curious Can-can

"I can do this."

"I am uniquely designed to do what only I can do."

"I can do anything, by the grace and strength of God, that He propels me into."

How often do you think about the word **can**[1] first thing in the morning? It's not potent enough to be dropped in the gutter like an F-bomb, but it's not the makings of a tender serenade either. It's not on any list of fifty most meaningful one-word tattoos to have etched with flowers or daggers on the side of your neck. (I know. I've checked.) Mostly, *can* is a workhorse quietly doing its job without fanfare. I think it's due for a little unpacking.

Simply put, *can* proclaims that we're capable of doing something. Think about your favorite pro in the NBA who can dunk with ease. Their blend of natural athleticism, serious practice and endless dreaming about the craft day and night. There's a tangible reality that he *can* make a shot, right? A man-sized hobbit like myself can dunk too—if it's out back in a dunking contest with all the third-graders in the neighborhood. I can totally destroy that Little Tikes hoop!

When those twelve disciples who walked with Jesus wrote to other

Christ followers, they spent time encouraging them to "walk by faith and not simply with their senses"[2] in order to intimately know "His incomparably great power for those who believe."[3] The twelve inform and remind others that they not only have access to the power of God here in the flesh, but that they are divinely set apart so that they can live lives utilizing His power in everything they do.

That message resounds today. I *can* engage the power of God.

Lately I've been waking up in an anxious fog. As my eyes open, I feel the cold weight of negative self-talk settle on my chest like a undesirable cat. For as long as I can remember, this same fog has crept in from one season to the next. Often it hovers in the next room, biding its time while giving me just enough space to catch my breath. It's not interested in a swift death, but a slow crush. Each morning it hijacks my rhythm and hangs around like an Ohio winter.

Making coffee? Yawn.

Reading Scripture? Too deep.

Drinking coffee? Bitter.

Eating peanut butter on waffles? Paste on cardboard.

Writing? About what?

Drinking more coffee? Whatever.

"I'm designed and skilled and filled with the Spirit. I can." Ah, now that changes things.

Maybe *can* is supposed to be one of those rallying words first thing in the morning. *Can't* sighs deep, disappointed and angry. *Can't* struggles to say good morning. But *can* echoes freedom as I push the cat off the bed. *Can* changes things.

I don't have to look to the past as soon as I'm conscious in the morning. I can look forward to the beauty of creation awaiting my incomplete but intentional adventure. I can co-create the journey ahead.

/ / /

Being a **co-creator**[4] is an interesting reality to explore. Humanity was created, is created, in God's image. Somehow we're like Him. We're a strange and unique blend of physical substance and a mental, emotional and spiritual nature. Because He creates and you and I are made to be like Him, we create. I think this explains why my heart wells up watching my kids' creativity in action. It's the overflow of a Creator-God on display in their lives.

Songs are a great demonstration of this co-creating. Songs are brought into existence. They're born out of context and culture. We feel them. Hear them. Sing them. Cover them. Personalize them. Yet even the most original songs are created out of the existence of notes and sounds that have been produced from the beginning of it all.

Making a baby, an unparalleled act of co-creation, shares similarities with songwriting. After all, some of the most heartfelt songs are born out of deep-seated relationships. Marriage is as unique a relationship as there is—the steady rhythm of a husband mingling with the graceful melody of a wife. And it's in the mess and miracle of that divine relationship, between two created beings, that a child is co-created. A new song is born.

Kids are naturally **curious**[5] too. The divine notes playing their individual tunes are the overflow of God's own melody. A melody full of diversity, wonder and divine curiosity. And that curiosity is a potent elixir for the soul. It cuts through the fog.

Several years ago I stumbled across a curious book at a small oceanside bookstore in the Outer Banks. Page after page detailed famous authors' quirky writing habits. It rocked me. I started settling into my own creative habits, like spending time in Scripture and prayer before writing a single word. Like making exactly six cups of Breakfast Blend before the sun creeps up. Like wearing a thrift store sport coat while creating.

Which made me think about how parents are like artists. Quirky co-creators. Some of us are more curious than others, of course. Some moms paint with broad strokes, while some dads listen for the singular tuning of each one of their kids. And some parents think creativity is a waste of time.

Since reading that book with my feet in the sand, this rhythm of curious habits has washed over all sorts of other compacted and compartmentalized mounds in my life. Like how I engage my wife. After more than a decade of marriage, with several kids underfoot, that curious hunger to encounter the individual Brooke with her melodic thoughts and colorful feelings, her personal visions and divine purpose, well, it had begun to dissipate. I don't recall feeling the invisible bond wear thin, but at some point, for convenience I guess, I tucked her deep within the incredible but incomplete role of "my wife."

"Hi, Lavar. I'd like you to meet Brooke, my wife. Oh look! Is that nacho cheese?"

It's awful isn't it? I don't think I'm alone in this.

When this concept of living curiously as a lifestyle began to intrigue me, to observe God's creation with awe and a sense of mystery, it struck me that while I had begun to overflow with joy at the curiosity and boldness of my kids, I had suppressed the wonder of Brooke. I had ceased to wonder at the God-breathed design of the woman He entangled me with. I think you know what I mean.

I couldn't recall small but vital elements about her. Like her favorite color. Marmalade orange? Flamingo pink? Oyster tan? Why is oyster tan even available?

What about her favorite restaurant? Taco Bell? Was it ever Taco Bell? High school dudes love Taco Bell at 2:00 a.m. on the weekend. Brooke is not a high school dude.

Dream job? Catering to my delicate constitution? What the heck was I thinking!

And what on earth was Jesus teaching her lately? I couldn't say. It was as though our season for marital curiosity had run its course. Case closed. I had passed the test, and as proof, we celebrated my high score with a wedding ceremony. Skip the studies. Let's make out then eat some nachos.

But then I began to wonder about her again. That kind of curiosity that rolls you over in a sweaty mess at night. Steps a little harder on the gas pedal on the drive home from work. Stops and stares for an awkward moment too long.

I think this is a piece of what it means to "become one flesh."[6] To be as curious about Brooke and her set-apart design as I am about God's work in me. To cover her with the love and truth of Creator-Christ at my own expense. To co-create a new and vibrant song so powerful that it surpasses sound, producing a radiant light that dispels the fog, enlightens the path, and fuses us together.

/ / /

Turns out, I want that air of curiosity. I want to live it and breath it. I want to quietly co-create alongside Brooke and our curious kids. I can do this. I actually can live this curious life through the power of Christ who strengthens and wisens me. I can raise my bandera high and chase after it. I can.

How about you? When was the last time you sat curiously pondering the next season? Did you bury your curiosity in the sand years ago? Listen, if you did, it's still there just below the growing dune. Dig. Dust it off. Imagine what can be in your faith, your marriage, your vocation. Maybe it's time to gird up your soul and co-create again. You can do it. You really can.

D

Doomsday

Discernment[1] isn't a word used around town all that often. It's such a deep word too. When was the last time you heard this particular word used at work? From a politician, a doctor, or a pastor? How about from your own lips in response to your kids?

Discernment is that divine ability to judge well. It roots deep and vines into healthy decisions and dreams. Like wine, it holds lingering notes of wisdom and truth with an elusive yet divine warmth laced throughout.

If you're not aware by now, I'm a dad. I love being a dad. It's a role that I find challenging and terrifying and righteous. Some days I fall asleep knowing that I nailed it. I put my head on that bamboo pillow beside my bride and acknowledge that I shared all I had to offer that day, either through the joy of a teachable moment or the discipline of an off-the-mark decision. Then there are nights I collapse in a heap after a day of short fuses and shorter vision. I lay there wondering why I was given so much power and influence over fresh souls with so little ability.

I'm realizing that more and more discernment rests on a foundation of divine truth. Discernment cuts through the noise. It muffles the negative chatter in my mind, if only for a moment, pushing back on the lies that insist I'm not skilled enough, ripped enough or spiritual enough. It stands firm against that despairing drone. You know the one: "Time to tuck that beard between your legs and hit the road, Rich. They'd all be better off without you. Go on, run! That's about all you have to offer, man."

Discernment knows better. When I toss and turn and tantrum, it matter-of-factly breathes Paul's ancient bandera: "Rich, if you have any encouragement from being united with your Rescuer, if any comfort from his love, any fellowship with the eternal Spirit, any tenderness or compassion, then make my joy complete by being like-minded, one in spirit and purpose. And don't be a selfish jerk. After all, your attitude should be like Jesus's."[2]

But discernment doesn't merely fight lies and battle demons, it raises a bandera. It presses me to call out and celebrate the victories of the day. Something mysterious happens when I pause to celebrate a win, even a minor win, like not eating cheese puffs after dinner or finishing this chapter on schedule. My heart and mind relax. Or maybe they temporarily unite. Whatever the case, a touch of peace settles the score and yields to a deep breath. I'm increasingly convinced that wisdom celebrates victories and shares that peace with Brooke in the quiet of the night.

And not only my victories, but the victories of those around me as well. Seems so obvious, doesn't it? To celebrate Brooke and the kids and our friends and family. Pouring hymn-like adoration over their success builds a crazy strong foundation, and it seems to have a reciprocal effect. It's amazing the joy that emanates from Elias when we celebrate his personal victories—a deeper understanding of fractions, an offer to pray at a large family dinner, his volunteering to do that job nobody else will. Watching my kids light up through the loving grace of a discerning word changes the game. Who doesn't like a high-five to the soul?

I think I'm understanding Paul's words more and more as I pull up my big-boy pants in this area of my life. He says, "Rich, I pray that your love may abound more and more in knowledge and depth of insight, so that

LEXICON OF AWESOME

you will be able to discern what is best and remain pure and blameless until Christ returns."[3] Love really does overflow through discerning words and actions. We all feel it too. It snuggles in close, even when it pinches.

/ / /

Just so you know, I'm not naturally an upbeat guy. My outlook on all things often begins with a **doomsday**[4] approach, after which I exhaustively work the reverse, attempting to discern fact from fiction. *Doomsday* is one of those dramatic words that really has no bearing on my daily life. It's an extreme word, isn't it? Like *holocaust* or *megadeath* or *genocide*. We're talking catastrophic destruction and unbelievable suffering.

Remember in the original *Ghostbusters* that part in the mayor's office after the ghost incarceration facility is forced to shut down? You know, when all hell breaks loose and the Ghostbusters frantically describe the end of the world in biblical proportions. As a kid, I was terrified at the thought of ghosts swarming like bees, life careening toward the end of it all with dogs and cats living together. Doomsday scenarios, right?

Doomsday in Ohio, however, often takes on the guise of cancer or divorce or an overdose. They seep in like cultural marxism and "pro-choice." Our doomsdays' pull us into the muck, stir up a deep fog and drop another bomb. Armageddon? Not quite. Instead, they're often internal, spraying shrapnel across the width and breadth of our souls. They break hearts and relationships and bodies.

I don't know the bombs dropped on your parade, beneath your bandera, but I do know that discerning the divine work of patience in the haze of fallout is a life-saving practice. I know it from experience. Though planted at ground zero, patience, when allowed to take root and wrap like a grapevine around our spirits, promises to produce fruit on the other end. Like Job, we stumble and stagger to the ash pit eager to cling to our compassionate Savior. We long to persevere.

For me, the Ohio doomsday demon is hidden somewhere between the Ghostbusters of my childhood and that self-deprecating whisper in my mind. He lurks in the hall just beyond the bedroom door, waiting to oppress and snatch and frustrate. He stalks in the next aisle, condemning and squeezing, gleefully wiping all confidence from my heart.

I don't think we're designed to carry that sort of weight day in and day out. I know millions of people around the globe do, and it's heartbreaking, isn't it? Doom is not God's intended position of the soul, which is why Creator Christ's rescue is so vital and worth every song we write Him in despair. There's something comforting about the melancholy of a song groaning with burdens relieved. And while life is full of minor chords, doom isn't intended to be our root note.

In fact, it's both the dread of feeling doomed in the grocery store aisle as well as the hope of what could be alongside Brooke that continues to push me to reengage life with purpose. To discern what's best here in the dirt. Now that's an idea to pack a tobacco pipe with and smoke on the front porch. **Diligence**[5]. to care about what we're putting our energy and time and treasure into, to work hard and persevere on purpose.

We celebrate with those who, by the grace of Creator God, persevere and overcome, if only for a moment longer. Their stories challenge us to the core. These people, from war heroes to cancer survivors to spouses breaking from abuse—they steal our breath, they tug on our hearts and they kick us in the butts. And they're all around us.

They're those faithfully diligent neighbors the author of Hebrews writes about. Men and women who have "conquered kingdoms, administered justice and gained what was promised"[6] through sacrifice and perseverance in the fog of doomsday. Though tortured, mocked, flogged, chained, and put in prison, these neighbors boldly "quenched the fury of the flames, and escaped the edge of the sword."[7] Their "weakness was turned to strength," and they "became powerful in battle"[8]—battles with swords, words, and thoughts.

Diligence—that discerning care for the work at hand in the face of a real and present doomsday. This is the mindset I want to wake up with. Don't you?

/ / /

Discernment reminds me that while my diligent work may not be rewarded in the flesh to the degree I desire, I can still move forward in purpose. Why? Because life is found in those deep breaths between struggle and victory.

How about you? In the midst of a doomsday, are you discerning your next move? I often wonder how much of the attitude of my mind spills over onto those under my roof. Do they feel the whispers of my personal doomsday? No doubt I'd rather they sense the curiosity and wonder of a new day. How about your kids? Do you chase them off in despair or draw them close as you discern the way forward? Let's discern together.

E

Endlessly Elemental

I watched shadows of clouds sprint through the old parking lot across the street and it struck me how endless they were. Not that those particular clouds would circle the globe for eternity, but that none of it ever really stops. Clouds whipping by in spring will morph into an unbearably humid summer, at which time I'll swear to install central air one day. Even those several weeks of sweaty, sleepless nights will inevitably become cool evening walks in parks under golden leaves. And, of course, those leaves will fall into snow. An eternal rotation of the seasons under a Northeastern sky.

There's something a little unsettling about the idea of **endless**[1], isn't there? It's terrifying in that awesome fear of God sort of way, yet warm and comforting in that Father God is with me in the gutter kind of way. Ongoing, eternal, without end. This whole concept is mind-blowing.

The other day I was connecting with a guy twenty years my senior who was wrestling with the reality of a changed season in his life. Not that life hadn't changed for him up to this point, but this present season, this latest surge of whipping winds, was most definitely more profound and personal than others had been. Like a winter proving to be particularly long. The clouds blowing past him were more biting than previous years. Shadows lingering in the dirt between erratic sprays of light had become disorienting. He noted how weak he felt in this season, exposed. Something needed to change.

The season would come to an end. Of course it would, that's what seasons do. But in the moment, he wasn't convinced the next would offer any more life and liberty. Listening to him speak, it struck me how, regardless of age, unexpected abnormalities can upend a relatively dull rhythm of life.

Endless sounds about as enjoyable as a root canal when eternity is clouded by struggle and confusion. *Endless* rings divine, however, when the bandera waves far ahead of humble adventure and deepening love. I don't think we can avoid wrestling with those long, cold winters that blow in, but maybe we can begin prepping our attitudes for them well in advance. Maybe we should tuck a few healthy, but abnormal, motivation bombs into our winter coat pockets.

/ / /

Seasons are defined by their unique **elements**[2] that impact our individual patches of dirt. Elements like billowing snow and boiling humidity. Blue sky and thick fog. Drought and the flood. Hurricanes and a wicked frost. Not only are these natural events rad band names, they also paint a broad picture of a season in action.

Seasons of life offer their own distinct elements, kind of like personal weather patterns. Youth offers immature risk, bold friendships, and crazy amounts of learning. Young life fosters fearless adventure with untamed attitude in expanding discovery. Adulthood grows beards and babies and heavier banderas.

Anomalous elements creep in too.

I remember coming out of a particularly long and brutal season of depression—my own version of doomsday, I suppose. It was as if I'd become another person for months, weak and fragile, like my endless-winter friend. I watched this me-like puppet from a distance, through a fog on the other side of a distorted window, brush off his kids, mope past his wife and sigh those deep and awkward sighs at the dinner table.

Then eastern winds blew in with a new sunrise. They tore apart the fog like a dog on meat, caused some tears and gasps and then filled my soul with an unexplainable **encouragement**[3] from the divine. It often happens this way in the throes of a funk. A sudden and tangible reminder that the Spirit of truth is near. Jesus leaning in, whispering, "Rich, you know Him. The Spirit lives with you and will be in you. Listen, I haven't left you as an orphan. I'll come to you before long."[4]

My shoulders lifted high, my chin raised higher, like in that painting of Washington crossing the Potomac. I could see past the haze and into the future again. I could breathe without feeling like it might be my last. In fact, breathing deeply felt crisp and cool, how I imagine the aftermath of a miracle to feel.

As a husband and a dad, I want stability. I want to live it, share it and breathe it, but I have to work with the heap of flesh that I am, right? My version of humanity in God's image is a different kind of broken than yours with different elements and encouragements.

I'm learning that my endless cycle of action to funk to divine motivation has pushed me to learn how to manage and move past my own limitations in order to risk failure and find success as the spiritual leader of my home and a coach to those discovering their own elements in changing seasons.

But it's not just the other side of funk that spurs me on. Chatting over coffee and laughing through bagels with my kids pushes me to grasp my dream. These one-on-one connects about life and faith and creative pursuits—well, they're a constant motivator for living a better version of my family rhythm, my faith and even my profession. It's amazing what kids stir up in the gut when they aren't brushed aside. Turns out, everyone cycles through seasons, even my kids, and I'm convinced that inspiration is tucked deep inside the particular elements that comprise our seasons, whether great or grief-ridden. And just as the Holy Spirit sidles up to me in the fog, with coffee in hand I get to do the same with those around me.

/ / /

Elias[5] was in kindergarten when we kicked off our rhythm of dad-son connects. "Dad, you spend time every week with those guys," he said, referring to some young dudes I had been discipling on different nights of the week. "When are you gonna do that with me?" That was it. That was all that needed to be said. I credit his earnest question early on as the catalyst for these regular connects that now include my oldest daughter and will eventually involve my youngest cutie as well.

YHVH is God.

YHVH is my God.

That's Elias, or at least that's what his name represents. He's our firstborn, and when I finally met him, I felt that thing deep inside that new parents feel. That powerhouse kick in my gut full of wonder and terror. Holding him, it was clear that I was full-on engaged in one of the most divine adventures I would ever embark on. More than a choice, Elias's birth proclaimed that YHVH is the Living Creator of all that is and was and ever will be, seen and unseen, womb to tomb. His birth was an aha moment. It was the exact opposite of everything a doomsday has to offer, exhilarating and life-giving. He, along with Ada and Joanna, are the incredible fruit that is the overflow of life with my co-creator, my wife.

But my kids aren't the flag I wave high in the air for all to see. No, they're beside me, feet in the dirt, hand in hand. The bandera of dreams waving high is a call to Christ-likeness. It's above and beyond all of my daily micro dreams and it completely shapes my God-breathed rhythm of life.

How about you? What season are you engaged in? What elements shape and define what God is doing in your life here and now? Spend some time journaling through past seasons, and where you can, connect the dots. After all, you never know when winter might chill your bones or spring burst into your soul.

F

Funtastic

I know, I know. **Funtastic** isn't a word. It's one of those amalgamations combining two pretty darn good words for the creation of a Franken-term expressing something unique. More and more, I think I understand this need to create something new out of the old in order to express something that feels inexpressible. I think most of us know what this is like on some level.

So, instead of disparaging a word as charming as *funtastic*, let's explore the root words and see where they take us. Who knows, maybe we'll walk away melding together a host of new expressions unique to our own experiences with our kids. New lexicons in full swing.

Fun[1] is a Jekyll-and-Hyde word. I can go out and have fun with my wife, or I can go ahead and make fun of her. I can enjoy her in one of her fun moods, or I can ratchet up a disagreement for a "real fun" evening together. I can't put my finger on it, but there's something unsettling about that sort of fun. I've heard about this sort of fun family reunion too. You know, the kind where fun dies on the dance floor while choking on a deviled egg between your drunk uncle and that shady second cousin twice removed. I've fed my fair share of fun-eaters. Fun-eaters are those monsters whose actions and whispers in dark seasons chew up fun simply because they prefer the taste of bitter tears over sugary sweet lovins. They fatten up on drama in place of burning calories through deep-bellied laughter. I've been that fun-eater too. It's not fun. Not in the best sense of the word.

When I'm saddled by the fake baggage of keeping up with the Joneses, or Progressives outrageous demands, or negative self-talk, the fun-eater is lurking. When I'm clear-minded and self-controlled, the fun-eater is at bay, bored and unsatisfied. And when the old fun-monster isn't happy, I probably am.

Soon after marriage, Brooke and I spent time on staff at a summer camp outside of Mad City. It was an awesome season with the full meaning of the word behind it. During summer camp with the young adult staff and volunteer high schoolers, we implemented the brilliant **fundatory**— mandatory fun. (F-words make for great amalgamations.) Fundatory was a simple, if not mildly dictatorial, way to foster staff bonding and help us experience something new beyond the mission while sharing life together for a season. It seemed like a good idea at the time, and to most of the summer staff it had the desired impact. For those who didn't quite catch the silly but genuine desire behind it, though, the flavor was a little less fun and bit more mandatory.

There are a lot of factors to consider to explain why fundatory wasn't a smash hit with everyone. Looking in from the outside, a few summers removed and a handful of kids of my own now, I imagine it has something to do with the loss of freedom of choice. Fun seems to lose its appeal when someone else decides what is and isn't fun for us. In hindsight it couldn't more obvious. Classic fun-eater scenario.

Yet, fun is almost always a choice, isn't it? Even when it doesn't seem like it. Growing up with a lot of trees on half an acre, raking was a beast. My siblings and I would spend hours moving leaves from one place to another, and every fall it happened again. No sooner would the leaves drop than I'd hear, "Richard, go help the others clean up the yard." Of course I didn't want to. Nobody wanted to. Until the pile was big and deep enough to drop ten feet from a branch into. Then leaf raking would be fully redeemed, a fundatory experience. Until those leaves lost their poof and the roots beneath the emaciated pile jammed their gnarled knuckles into unwitting children's spines.

I'm not responsible for entertaining my kids twenty-four hours a day, that's not my job. No parent should take on that burden. However, as a dad attempting to pass on the mindset of Christ, I get to challenge those momentary whines with new sets of lenses for my kids to see their circumstances through when they're stuck in the chain gang of my decisions. "You can stay disappointed, or you choose to see this as a God-breathed opportunity for a challenging adventure you didn't expect."

No doubt you can think of a few (thousand) people who might find a fresh sense of purpose by grabbing ahold of this type of mindset. I know I can. I've been one, for sure.

Most of that Mad Town summer camp team rolled into fundatory like it was their destiny. They owned it. They ate cheese curds at the market, downed brats at Brat Fest like it was, well, Brat Fest, and spit out sunflower seed at the Mallards stadium with vengeance. I like to imagine they even left camp with a greater sense of freedom on mission when the season closed out.

/ / /

Freedom[2] is one of those words I've taken for granted. I live in the freest society ever to exist on planet earth since that naked couple in that ancient garden. I have the freedom to worship my God. I'm free to wear my favorite pair of jeans. Free to work as much as I'd like, save my money and move to where I'd rather be. Free to learn the skills necessary to develop a career of my choosing, to mature as a husband

and to grow as a father. I'm free to avoid paths that lead to addiction and free to run from abuse. I'm free to raise that bandera high. And I have no doubt that you could add a dozen more elements to that list without hesitation.

Sounds terrifying and exhilarating, doesn't it? The journey into freedom, in fact, almost always trudges through the muck of doomsday time and again. It's as though freedom costs something. As if sacrifice were deeply connected to liberty.

"It's for freedom that Christ has set you free, Rich. Stand firm in your freedom and don't let yourself be burdened by the chains of slavery again."[3] Such a simple point, isn't it? Paul wants his audience, the Church, to understand that Christ's sacrifice was for our freedom— freedom from the slavery of sin and self-sabotage and the fun-eater. This divine freedom isn't just *from* evil but *for* all the righteous awesomeness that comes with freedom. Freedom is *forward*, not just *from*.

Healthy freedom and healthy fun have something in common: boundaries, sacrifice and insight. Like playing the sexiest instrument ever to rise out of the forest, the bass guitar. Until I learned notes and scales and rhythm and tuning and orchestrating with other musicians, I was trapped in my little world of noodling around. It was only once I sacrificed time in other areas of life and put in the work to grow in skill and experience that I discovered the freedom to play more. I developed more styles, honed my technique and collaborated with more people in unexpected places. Freedom. And with it came the opportunity to have fun. I'm watching my kids do this now with their instruments and arts and ideas.

It's sort of like the process of casting a new vision or developing new goals. There's always an initial step of releasing unnecessary bonds in order to allow our imagination space to wander. Most of us, my kids included, need an invitation or a primer in order to dream beyond the immediate. Once we have it, though, we are divinely set up for the tangible work of freely envisioning our **fantastic**[4] **future**[5]. Two more F-words for your lexicon.

Who do I want to be? Where do I want to go? How has God wired me? What could I do with my talents and skills while on earth? What else could there be? The visions these questions foster are beyond our immediate ability to realize. That's the nature of fantastic, though. Born out of unrestrained imagination, these visions challenge our current beliefs about who we are and usher us into extravagant fantasies about what life could hold. With shackles gone, we can aim for the heavens.

The future almost always seems fantastic if you think about it. It's out there, and we're still back here trying to catch up. I think that's what makes the journey so much fun, so challenging and inviting.

It's uninhibited imagination which spills all over the gritty work of our current reality, weaving our bandera beyond the horizon. Here and now we begin the process of connecting the dots between the dirt and the dream.

Do you know how hard this is? Of course you do.

I'm discovering that most adults have a hard time dreaming. I mean *really* envisioning a bold future beyond their current finances, attitudes, body weights, vocations, family dynamics and anything else pricking their soul. The weeds of everyday life tangle up and choke out the adventure. The freedom to dream fades like an ancient, forgotten art form. Or worse, it's tossed aside in resentment, like fundatory by those students who missed its purpose. Or like picking up a bass guitar twenty years later and forgetting how to tune and walk and listen.

On the other hand, some of us have a hard time keeping our feet on the ground. Our heads are so far up in the clouds we're dizzy from a lack of oxygen.

Years ago, I spent a month at a four-day seminar on healing old wounds.

The speaker talked about how we need to learn to build a bridge between our physical and emotional states through our "sanctified imagination." Doesn't that just grab your adult mind and give it a good bear hug? Sanctified imagination is a simple meditative journey of imagining what it would be like to join Christ in releasing and redeeming our deep hurts and debilitating baggage. It's another way of describing the freedom God offers us to live with hope, to dream big dreams beyond the now and allow the Creator space to ignite our imaginations from a healthy launching pad.

/ / /

Watching my kids, it seems obvious that we're designed to imagine life beyond our present circumstances. That we're created to become enamored with the heavens from our perch in the soil. In fact, I'm convinced that if we're going to imagine a better future for ourselves, for our kids, for our communities and tribes, we've got to learn to do so with one foot in the orchard and one in the muck of our undeveloped field.

So, what does freedom look like in this season for you? Is it physical? Emotional? How about mental—freedom in your mind from those thoughts that keep haunting you? Imagine how funtastic it would feel to wake up wholly free tomorrow or next month or this time next year. Maybe it's worth adding a little fundatory to your family rhythm.

G

Oh So Good

I have this **good**[1] friend in the Upper Midwest. He's one of those guys who carries around a bank of goodwill everywhere he goes. Everyone who knows him smiles and nods when his name comes up. Of course, like the storybook man that he is, he humbly passes every ounce of good credit on to the Creator. Sounds like something Jesus would have done.

This is not my default. I don't naturally haul around cluster bombs of goodwill toward men. My arms get tired.

There it is. Did you see what I did there? I think it's something most of us do. Maybe it's a self-defense mechanism. Maybe it's an attempt at humorous self-deprecation. It might even be authentic self-discernment. Whatever the root, it's awkward when it happens.

You felt it, didn't you? That suppression of belief in the goodness of God in my own life? Of course it's good for me to step back and evaluate my own life rhythm. Mature adults do this often. It's sobering. I compare my story with the stories of families suffering in the underground church or girls freed from the modern slave trade or kids who sacrifice their birthday cash for disaster relief. "Man, those are good people," I want to say. "They really live and breathe the love and truth of God." There's a beneficial self-awareness that can come with filtering your story along with others' through God's gracious light.

However, the "I don't naturally carry around that much goodwill," half-mumbled, pity-filled one-liners? They don't just steal some light, they snuff it out.

"Dad, tonight I'm going to make bracelets for all my friends," said Ada bouncing down the sidewalk after school, shining bright.

"How many?"

"Um, I think five. I wanna give one to everyone I've been playing with at recess." Her excitement was contagious. At least, it would have been to a dad not immunized with skepticism and funk.

"Five!" I choked in place of, "You're so generous!" or "What a great idea!"

"Well, I've got one started already and I..." Light beginning to quiver.

"Tonight's chore night, and we have to run some errands after dinner. You have homework too, right? What about reading? You still have a few chapters to hammer out. I hope you didn't promise these for tomorrow." Light officially snuffed out.

I think situations like this happen when I look away from that divine bandera, when I forget about the journey and the travelers I'm entrusted with. Whatever the cause, I'm pretty sure goodness doesn't mumble in half-hearted gloom with snuffer in hand. No, goodness steps into the light, embodies its source, then refracts it onto others. Bracelets take form in the light, not the smoke.

"Well, at least I'm not a genocidal maniac." If you've made this proclamation, it's safe to say your bandera's not waving high enough. Goodness zeroes in on Christ and His character. He's where all eternally good comparisons and measurements take shape. Hitler? It's a lose-lose, even if it's an easy win. Of course I'm not Hitler, even if I do manage to muck up my fair share of life. I don't want to look good next to Hitler. I want to be good in the rhythm and rhyme of Christ.

But does this conversation even matter? After all, if Jesus wouldn't personally accept the title "good teacher" when offered it but instead, like my Midwestern friend, refracted all goodness to Father God, isn't this personal goodness discussion a waste of time?

No. No, it's not.

Christ gave all glory to God, and He still does. Like I said, I don't naturally carry around goodness, but I do supernaturally wear it like a bathrobe. Bathrobes are luxurious, they're utilitarian and they cover from head to toe, and God's qualities, His traits, His essence adorns us likewise. Christ fills believers, you and me, with His Holy Spirit, and that Spirit fills us with His supernatural fruit, of which goodness is one gracious gift. We radiate His glory. And you know what? If you ask me on a good day, I'll respond like Jesus, "No, no, I'm not good. Only God is good. If you see any goodness in and through and around me, understand that it's the Holy Spirit weaving a sweet bathrobe of grace just my size."[2]

/ / /

I suppose that's where **grace**[3] comes to light. God intervenes as I stumble in the shadows, tripping over my own funk and falling headfirst into the muck. No matter how much wallowing I do, He invites me to grab hold of His rhythm of life. He lets me in on His ancient lexicon and the rhyme of it all. I'm not the most worthy dude on earth. I don't deserve this constant attention from the Living God. But that's my point; that's the essence of grace, isn't it? Something beautiful and joyfully given without merit. Unearned. Undeserved.

I don't deserve Brooke's promised and faithful love. Despite that, her rhythm of life involves offering it to me daily through gentle caresses down my back, through hushed words each morning before our two-year-old appears at the bottom of the stairs and through patience as I trip my way through difficult seasons of depression. Grace is both unseen and tangible and here and now.

My friend in the Upper Midwest offers grace like a family meal. It's there for the stranger in line at the café just as it is for close friends weathering storms. It's free too. No, not in that creepy-cultish "drink this and follow me into utopia" kind of way. It's more natural, like befriending a stranger you feel you've known your whole life. Sure, offering authentic grace may seem a little awkward at first, but divine grace is uncomfortable if not offensive in its fullness. Yet when the meal's through, we always thank the chef and enjoy dessert.

It seems as though goodness and grace run in the same circles, sort of like birthdays and presents. Birthdays are funtastic celebrations of life and growth and value. Perennial opportunities for adoration. And the **gifts**[4]? The overflow of grace.

Of course my kids don't deserve the gifts they receive. They're hardly perfect little creatures. But presents aren't given with a note dangling from the ribbon stating, "You don't deserve this. I'm giving it to you because I'm good. Period." To be honest, as a quasi-adult, I'm keenly aware of this little nugget of reality before a gift ever hits the table. No, gifts arrive under the banner of joy and pleasure and this divine sort of endowment that consumes the moment. I want to show my traveling partners how thankful I am that they're mine and breathing another day and loved by the Gift Giver on purpose.

You and I, moms and dads, our gifts are offered to our kids beyond the present. We celebrate their advent right here in their current state of maturity while looking forward with eternal hope to who they will become.

/ / /

Not long ago I heard someone say that saving for retirement is a gift to my future me. I needed to hear that. This is one of the motivators behind my adventures in life coaching—this idea that if we make gritty decisions today to clarify who we want to be, what we hope to accomplish, and in what direction we'd love to journey, our future selves will thank us.

I can imagine an old, future Rich, traveling back in time to offer a young Ricky advice.

"Hey," old me says with a hushed, sage-like voice, "that pastoral ministry role you're exploring? Not happening."

"Wait, what ministry? Where?"

"But it's a worthy investment. We'll learn a ton, and it'll launch us down the coaching road."

"So I'm pouring all my energy into a non-starter?" young me says with obvious hesitation.

"Those trips and bruises built our character, young man," said the bearded sage. "We discovered a depth of insight and investment often overlooked."

"Why would God allow me to wander down this road for so long?"

"That's a good question. I've asked myself the same thing," said future me with a subtle smile. "Just remember, He's an eternal investor. He plays the long game, and in the end, so will we. Dream big, my friend. Dream big."

Your future you has received the gift of your willingness to imagine what could be, your boldness to act and your Christlike perseverance in holding to an honest bandera of dreams. How does it feel to hand yourself such a deeply rewarding gift?

 It's safe to say that our gritty, truth-filled work today and tomorrow offers the best chance of joy-filled success next month and next year. I think our kids need to witness this too. They need to experience it along with us. They need to peek inside our journey, realize it's not an easy, privileged road and grasp the reality of persistence within delayed gratification.

On the other hand, I can imagine a future me showing up wearing the same clothes I'm wearing right now, smelling like the night before with an empty look in the eye.

"So what's life like one year from now?" I ask.

"Oh, ya know, still waiting on that perfect ship to sail up my river. To be honest, I don't think about it much anymore. Not even sure I care. I think I'm just gonna snuggle into our favorite pillow and watch *Hitch*, again. Got any cheese puffs or did we eat 'em all?"

"*Hitch* is great, but what about our studies? What happened to our goals?"

"Pffffft."

"Our dreams?"

"Deader than a possum on the freeway."

"And this coaching thing? What's up with that?"

"Coaching? As in Little League? We don't play ball. Hush now. Hitch is talking."

Future me pops the bag of cheese puffs and settles in.

"Oh, come on, man," he says, wiping cheese dust on his shirt, "don't cry. You don't realize how hard it is to keep that schedule going day after day after day. Sure there were hints of progress here and there, and I know, I know, it'll pay off one day, but the obstacles, man. They just wouldn't let up. One after another. Like the world is against me or something. Who cares. There's always next year, right?"

I just threw up a little in my mouth. I've lived that scenario more times than I have space to write about. It's unsettling. That's not a gift to my future me. No, it's a bomb wrapped up in a dirty bathrobe and slathered with the shrapnel of cheese puffs and disappointment. And it serves up disaster to everyone involved.

Goodness, the sort that surpasses the immediate and spills over into the future lives of those around us—this is worth the investment, right? Parenting is this sort of awesome reality lived out daily. Discipline today is a future gift to my kids. Completing chores and schooling with ethic and passing on faith and shaping a healthy lexicon are gritty habits worth their weight in the gold nuggets of future success.

If you could travel back in time just one year and have a cup of coffee with yourself, what would you say? Or imagine chatting with future you one year from today. What would you hope to hear? Sure, maybe the journey doesn't go as planned, but that's why God's grace is so vital. He offers it for the next season and the new bandera. He offers it to you and your kids.

What's next?

H

How the Hope?

"How did I get here?"

You've asked this, I know. Great questions often begin with **how**[1]. I think it's because these are curious questions, questions that lead to deeper and more profound observations. "How did I get here?" is a solid starting point.

Shift the focus and it becomes a great way to discover the life and times of someone sitting across the table.

How did you…?

How would you…?

How are you…?

See what I mean? It's this simple sort of reflection that instigates a deeper connection with my dude or my little lady. The stale "Did you finish your homework?" is traded for the mind-engaging "How did you figure out that elusive equation?" or "How can you put that knowledge to use at home?" How knocks on the door, hoping for an invitation to dinner.

And it's a simple way to push into the bowels of the discovery process too. These kinds of catalytic questions spark backyard wrestling matches between gut and soul.

"Rich, take a look at your schedule. If you had all the freedom in the universe, how would you change it?"

"Dude, how much of your free time would you be willing to sacrifice for grace and peace in that relationship?"

"How will you act on that opportunity by the end of the week?"

"Great idea! How about another…and another…and how about one more? Look at that, Rich, now you have several options to work with and no rocks to crawl under."

Peeling from the onion, I've come to realize that how is vital to fleshing out the lifeblood of the Great Commands of Creator Christ. How do I love God? How do I love myself? How do I love my neighbor standing shoulder to shoulder with me at the grocery store?

But better questions aren't easier questions. Better questions draw a melancholic out of his private cave, and their earnestness can be exhausting.

Sometimes I feel bad for Brooke. She navigates melancholy like a captain does a rocky coast. Which means she can discern the good exhaustion—divine service, hard work, fulfilling projects, play with the kids—from the bad exhaustion—negative self-talk and too much socializing. She recognizes how questions both coming in and going out are draining for a guy like me. Up to a point they're life-giving, but like too much of a good thing—even that good thing—things turn south without deep and meaningful refreshment.

No doubt I'm part of a tribe out there taking a deep breath and saying, "Yeah, yeah, I get it. That's me. I love being with others. I want to feel their stories and struggles and hopes. I need their shared faith and frailty. But I burn out so fast." Which points us to a better lexicon, right? We get to engage the aha! and ask, "How do I create a healthy rhythm of living the Great Commands without wiping out my spirit and family and deep friendships?"

How begins to connect the facts of today with our imagination of what could be out there in the future. It draws from hindsight and presses forward through insight.

Of course, sometimes I'd prefer to mutter a flippant "No!" but that wouldn't further the journey. *No* wouldn't push me to grow, and *no* doesn't answer a good how question. It's safe to admit that after years of doomsday dispersions I want depth with my bride. I want to foster possibilities of the imagination while igniting a sense of unity in love. For this to happen, I've got to dig a little deeper than my caveman-esque monosyllabism.

Yeah, these questions are risky. Great things are.

There's something humbling about curiosity, isn't there? Emotive King David sang that God "guides the humble in what is right and teaches them His way."[2] It's a vulnerable position to be in. The position of a person leaning into the guillotine. Knees bent, palms open, neck outstretched. Humility[3] is a risk.

On the other hand, being curious enough to **humble**[4] ourselves at the feet of another, even our Creator, is a mature posture. It means we're the one in the relationship who doesn't get it, who doesn't know, who is reliant on the other to complete the transaction and willing to bow. No doubt I need to bend a knee more often.

Thankfully, Brooke is just as attracted to the sight of a humble man crawling around in the dirt as she is my wrestle-a-badger-with-my-bare-hands bold strength. No doubt I spend more time facedown in the dirt these days. Ever wonder if this sort of humility is the overflow of the divine relationship that took form outside the walls of that ancient garden? Husband and wife starting fresh in fear and forgiveness. I can appreciate that man's confusion and pain in his call to lead on purpose through the unknown. There must have been a dance between the two—one humbling and encouraging and the other pressing on, flailing about and righteously rising up to another challenge, then vice versa. A genuine proto-display of "submitting to one another out of reverence for Christ."[5]

From the look of that guillotine posture, wisdom forms in the fray of humble hows and whats. As awesome to witness as it is to experience.

Truth is, if you're willing to ask how, then you're probably willing to listen.

If you're willing to listen, you're most likely willing to learn.

And if you're willing to learn, you're preparing to act.

Tied together, humility becomes a life of *how* in action, requiring patience, gentle inquiries, and intentional observations. Marriage lives in this realm. Ask Brooke. Through grit and growth, the tangible love of God bears the burden of humility deep in our bones on any given day, in any and every word and through every thought and deed within our walls. Isn't this exactly what Paul was emphasizing to those couples in Ephesus?

How do I love Brooke? "Well, start by loving her with the same sacrificial love Christ offered to the church."[6]

I've heard Paul's words. I've felt them. But maybe for the first time I'm curious about them. What does that Christlike love for Brooke actually look like? "Rich, it looks like a man choosing to present Brooke holy to God each and every day."[7] How do you lift up in holiness? With humble respect and honor and reverence. Through warm I love yous, daily dishwashing, pre-planned date nights and evening prayer.

/ / /

It's wild how quickly a humble heart and rhythm can be swallowed up by hurt. We use the phrase "hurt people hurt people" around our house. I don't know who coined it, but I first heard it from a professor years ago. My gentle wife learned it from Pastor Bob growing up. Pastor Bob is one of those godly men who can offer a lifetime of wisdom in a bite-size phrase. It's corny but clarifying, isn't it? And if Pastor Bob said it, then it's worth putting to memory.

Hurt[8] gives birth to hurt.

Isn't it interesting how the residue of an old wound will attempt to crash in like a rogue wave? Insert your own past hurt: _____. Do you feel it? Where I've suffered, even within the scope of absolute forgiveness and demonstrable healing, it's as though old emotional waves continue to crash around, waning for sure, yet still washing up on my shore from time to time. A salty splash of anguish without cause. And this suffering left internally untended bleeds out further and with greater mess, doesn't it?

When I feel like a failure in my vocation, that attitude spills over onto my kids as they attempt their homework. They begin their task with confidence and joy in the challenge until I show up deflated, open my mouth, and begin to speak the tongue of Mordor. Yeah, you know what I mean—those hurtful and completely unhelpful groans of "ought to" and "should have" and "why didn't you." Hurt people hurt people. It's a bloody mess.

Yet—and this is a huge yet—when I recognize this bloody mess for what it is and press all the more into the forgiveness birthed on the cross, I'm able to keep an eye on the shifting surf, look to that bandera drawing me upward, recognize the rampant emotional waves crashing in and step forward with a deep breath and solid stride. **Hope**[9] invigorates for the swim and refreshes for the marathon.

I think this is part of Christ's ongoing work of restoration. He absorbs the cosmic waves hurling through my emotional sea while washing off the salty residue from the unwarranted crash right here in my chest. Hope inspires endurance, overflows from faith and acts in humility. We can be "confident of this, that Creator and Healer God, who began a good work in you and me, that He's going to see it through to completion."[10] There's hope in those waves.

You and I, we don't have to remain helpless on shore. We're free to learn how to swim alongside Christ. We're free to sidle up next to our kids and teach them how to freestyle. We're free to team up with husbands and wives and friends and mentors and grasp life with bold humility. We're free to hope in action.

/ / /

Hurt people hurt people until they humbly ask, "How did I get here, what am I doing and how can I move forward?" Do this for a while and you'll find yourself in the discerning position of a curious observer in another's life, asking, "How did you get here? Where would you like to grow from here? What's God doing in your life here and now?"

How do you want to spend the next three years of your life? Defensive and drained or curious, humble and firing on your finest cylinders? Imagine how life might breathe if you were to shift from fostering and spreading hurt to humbly feeding your soul and offering hope to those around you.

Interesting Investment

Not long ago, it struck me that the questions I'm bold enough to ask are an **investment**[1] in my future. Ever think of your questions in this way? Or the curious questions our kids come up with and the impact their interest has on life and faith?

"Dad, how do guinea pigs survive in the wild?" isn't a life-altering question, but the threads attached to the driving curiosity and the response I give add to the depth of my kid's journey. And it's this sort of interest, even what appears to be pointless interest to an impatient parent, that develops into the building blocks for maturity later on.

"Lord, coaching stokes that smoldering soul fire within. Would you toss on a few more logs to warm a few more clients?" isn't as cuddly a question as the one about guinea pigs, but earnestly seeking divine guidance, with questions that stem from those unashamedly silly ones of the past, is an investment in my journey. I'm not convinced there's no such thing as a stupid question, but a curious one, no matter how many guinea pigs are involved, is another penny in the investment-question piggy bank. The investment-question piggy bank has a snowballing effect. As that piggy swells, so do our questions. And questions that boldly and curiously attempt to connect our current reality with our preferred future emblazoned on that high-flying bandera are investments. And investments fatten the pig.

When Moses met God in the burning bush, barefoot and curious, he asked, "Who am I?"[2] in what seemed like an attempt at dodging the call. This isn't your lofty, head-in-the-clouds, deeply introspective sort of wonder, but the classic "What do I have to offer?" self-deprecating sort of dispute. It's a bold question to ask Creator God at the center of a divine mystery in action in the wilderness. Dodgy or not, it's an investment that changed Moses's life forever. One that altered Israel's future from that point on.

Then there's Nehemiah's question to Artaxerxes: "If it pleases the king and if your servant has found favor in his sight, let him send me to the city in Judah where my ancestors are buried so that I can rebuild it."[3] The faith and guts to ask this powerful ruler, the man overseeing this overthrown people, Nehemiah's people, permission to leave with international protection and rebuild his ancestral kingdom—this is nation-changing, history-making stuff. That prayer-filled question, like Moses's, was an investment, not only in his own journey, but in the movement of Savior God.

Both Mo and Nehem engaged God in their present states for the sake of future possibilities. Questions seem to give birth to adventure. And adventure—wild, teary-eyed adventure—requires investment in the unknown. I'm discovering more and more that these sort of investments are ripe with the internal spiritual endowment of something bigger and better than my flesh can muster. I think that's what makes an adventure, wilderness to mountain peak, so valuable.

Asking questions with an honest desire to process and grow in all seasons of life is like that slow drip into a 401(k). Remember that future gift to yourself? Those hard decisions are deeply connected to this questioning process. Questions demand decisions. And our decisions become adventures. And adventures compound our investments.

I don't know when I first grasped an understanding of investing, but these days it's like brewing coffee. The hardest part is deciding which flavor sounds best. Questions are like the flavor of the day. Which one and how strong and how many cups. Only more personal. These curious questions build endless bridges between spirit and Spirit. It's an investment far greater than today's coffee or tomorrow's money.

I was thinking about the different parts of the word *investment* and trying to capture an image beyond throwing money at a bank. I wanted a better view of investing. A bigger imagination.

Dissecting the word, I began in the middle, hoping to cozy up with *vest*. I imagined a vest being bestowed upon me by my younger, sexier self. I slipped it on to hold me tight just beneath the skin, covering my heart and gut. A protective vest placed on my insides, the likes of something between Kevlar and that old-school red quilted lumberjack deal. Warm and death-defying.

Then I stepped back to the beginning to have a chat with the prefix *in*. *In* is a mechanical word. It's all about getting the job done, whatever that job is. Sort of the like the "fixer" or "cleaner" in a mob movie. It's available to make it happen and make it clear. Here *in* attaches itself to *vest* like a tight-knit, well, vest. Together they begin to weave a more enticing garment.

Finally, I grabbed the suffix, *ment*, to see how it's woven into this picture. *Ment* shows action, like when the vest is picked up, placed beneath the skin, and worn around town for a bit. An in-vest-ment.

But then I started to spiritualize it. I started to think how an investment is an internal adornment of something greater to come, vested with the benefits, power and protection of the future fulfillment. Christ invests in us. Christ fills us. He covers and surrounds us with His Spirit. And the more curious we are in this investment, the more depth of insight we experience. Questions foster this, don't they? Good questions, honest ones, dress us and prepare us for the future.

Of course, we invest in things all the time without realizing it. Binge-watching six seasons of Lost is an investment of time; it's just that the investment is low-risk with immediately unfulfilling, and most likely not-so-beneficial, rewards. I have a few of these daily investments lurking in the form of cheese puffs and politics.

Sitting on my porch, eating cheese puffs and feeling my chest for that internal vest, it struck me just how much I desire that vertical investment. How much I long to draw closer to Christ and all the kingdom benefits. I know, I know, it's a bit of a cliché Christian sentiment. Good thing for you I'm a dad. I breathe clichés. But it's an honest insight, and an ancient one too. Dads have felt this longing since the garden. It's universal, though I think it impacts us in different ways through different cultures and in different seasons—young dads with babies and old men with grandkids—but the same Spirit grips our hearts right through the vest, squeezes a bit, and stokes a new desire for what matters beyond the money, the vocation, the coffee and the Jones family next-door.

It's both comforting and startling how invasive this divine investment is in my daily rhythm.

/ / /

"If you're interested, you're interesting."

I met Brooke at a pool party. Many pool parties, actually. A summer full of them. And we met a little more each time. Each discussion would carry on a bit deeper into the night. One question after another as the dew settled and the stars stepped up for a show.

"So, where do you imagine life taking you after college?"

"How do you suppose God orchestrates meetings and mission?"

"What do you think it means to marry a friend above and beyond a romance?"

I first heard this idea that **interested**[4] makes interesting from a pastor in southern Ohio. I brushed it off at first, defensive I think, the effects of a low self-confidence. But in practice? Yeah, it seems right on the money. There's something about spending time with someone who is genuinely interested in our opinions, ideas, vocation, family, or faith that tends to foster a deeper and more meaningful connection. We feel safe and liked and worthwhile, reminded that we have something to offer the world.

When Brooke asked me a million questions about my family and my dreams and my journey with Christ, well, I went home convinced that she was the most interesting woman on the planet. Interesting because she offered an array of curious questions and intimate answers. Interesting because she cared, if only to build a bridge for the moment. Interesting because she invested in me.

Catch that?

Brooke's lifelong investment in her own faith built a bridge of genuine curiosity to mine. Her parents' investment in her personal growth years before we met fostered a confidence in her own journey and a divine interest in me. Her investments not only drew me in, but they set us up for an ongoing relationship overflowing with curious kids, a patchwork faith, and a unique bandera.

I think Jesus's simple response, "Love the Lord your God with all your heart, soul, mind and strength...and love your neighbor the way you show yourself love,"[5] is applicable to our interesting investment calculation here. A loving investment in God and self organically develops into a genuine curiosity about others and an investment in their wellbeing.

Connecting those dots is invigorating, isn't it? Just **imagine**[6] it. Yes, using our imaginations for healthy pursuits is vital to seeing that bandera wave. So imagine hearing that future divine greeting: "Well done, good and faithful servant."[7]

What do you think about investment in a Christlike rhythm of life? How do you feel about God's divine interest shining on you and your mission? How would you respond to that invigorating sense of freedom and victory at the sound of eternal God welcoming you into eternity?

Feels good, doesn't it? Like watching my kids' eyes light up when I greet them with a hug and genuine wonder about their day, their discoveries, their insight into this divine adventure. There's something mutually life-giving about tapping into Ada's heart and diving into Elias's mind. Everyone wins. And anyone in any season can do this.

As an aging introvert, I'm still developing and expanding this imaginative interest in others. Truth is, I am interested. I'm simply working on putting that interest into practice. That said, I'm convinced more and more that we're all designed to breathe life into someone else, to invest in a deeper engagement right where we stand. And you know what? Stirring up an invigorating interest in another while inviting the Spirit to stir our own soul is an investment with far-reaching implications.

/ / /

Whether you're asking, "Who am I?" or "How do I impact my kids for the long haul?" or "Why are guinea pigs so darn cute?" step back and observe what you're investing in. Who are you showing divine interest in? What investments are really causing the piggy to swell?

Maybe you simply need to spend time reinvigorating your family and friends. Which begs the question, what invigorates you in this season? After all, when you're invigorated, you're interested, and when you're interested, you're investing in your imagined future.

J

Go Ahead and Jump

To this day I feel a jolt of enjoyment sitting beside my youngest daughter watching lightning bugs materialize out of the dark. Nighttime unfolds like a blanket, releasing glow bugs for their survival and our pleasure. Joy seems to unfurl this way too.

Every morning at around seven-thirty, I listen in on Joanna's chatter through old plaster walls. Soon after, that soft voice moves ahead down the stairs until those divine little footsteps patter across the floor to my side. Little arms wrap and squeeze. The image of God overflowing with joy.

Joanna[1] fosters that deep pleasure within the Dyson crew. Maybe it's because she's named after both of her grandmas that joy is so apparent in her eyes and through her voice, a multigenerational trail of happiness flowing throughout her tiny body. Maybe it's my kick-butt parenting. Maybe it's her unique personality shaped by the Spirit. I suppose it's all the above and if you press me I'll add that God is the source of her joy, which then spills over onto everyone within smiling distance. I guess that's the gentle yet persistent quality of joy—that it forges divine trails through blood and faith.

Whatever the case, she oozes it.

Her smile evokes a sense of fulfillment and pleasure.

Her laughter draws Elias and Ada in close, asking for more.

In the dark moments of a doomsday funk, Joanna squeals with joy. When it's gray and heavy and the bandera of dreams is wrapped in fog, she materializes with a run and a hug. Like a miniature choir director, she rallies us to "Clap our hands and shout to God with cries of joy!"[2] By the grace of God, she carries a light beyond her awareness, shining with wonder and delight.

/ / /

What's interesting about **joy**[3] is that it seems to be connected to something beyond us, like a Joanna. Joy wells up at the thought of being somewhere desired or with someone loved. It engages our expectations and is impacted, to all sorts of varying degrees, by fear and hurt and anger.

The first time I read through the stories of Jesus, I had no particular expectation one way or the other of how I would think or feel afterward. While joy was growing around the edges, fear was folding in like yeast. I think I was scared to believe in something holy, someone all-powerful—a Creator who knew me in the womb, set parameters throughout the universe, breathed the life of the Spirit into my gully, and could rescue me from my doom and despair.

The same was true when I picked up the bass guitar. No, I didn't think that old Yamaha was holy and all-powerful, but I did fear it a little. I think I feared the expanse of possibility more than I understood its potential for joy.

Writing used to hold the same air about it. The first time I really put my hand to the keyboard in high school, a personal project without any parameters or expectations, I was terrified at the thought of someone's reading it, mocking it, and tearing me down for its existence. A different source of fear, sure, but still an experience over and above the hidden joy. Of course, I did share it with a buddy at school, and yes, he did tear apart the plot and the dialogue and the characters. What's more, he threw it down, stomping and laughing, only to set the pages on fire in the hallway. That's how I remember it.

I still have that sci-fi story in a bin of childhood memorabilia. Even now, years later, I feel the youthful jabs connected to it. I think that script and those memories carry the weight of an advent, the beginning of a chapter in my own story more than two decades ago.

These days, writing is a joy. I still fear the process of putting words to paper, though now it's that awesome sort of fear that expects Creator God to engage and offer insight. I write as a way of connecting my experiences to the ideas swimming around deep in my soul. I write so that I can move onto the next season. And I anticipate a joy-filled engagement in the struggle to find the word and the rhythm and the subject. The whole process is endowed with something beyond me, something divine.

Which brings me back to the story of Jesus.

Part of the wonder of Jesus's story is that it's both divinely terrifying and completely joy-filling at the same time. There's a sweet pleasure that emerges when I spend time with God in Word and prayer early in the morning. Coffee, front porch and the oceanic rhythm of the Psalms or the fast-paced story of Mark—these foster a divine enjoyment that lives beyond the moment, that hums along behind the scenes of the day.

These mornings, when "the word of Christ dwells deeply in my gut as I spill over in admonishment with the wisdom of God, grateful in the depths of my heart and giving thanks to the Father through Christ,"[4] I think the joy of Jesus, from progeny to Page, overwhelms. I look forward to it, and I feel off when I rush by it to launch the day.

We need the expectation of joy in our lives, maybe even as much as we need water and community and God. Yeah, it takes work to find fresh water in the wilderness, build deep and lasting friendships, and learn how to fully rest in God's truth, but it's worth it. And training our hearts and minds to expect joy around each corner is no different.

On the other hand, I think part of what makes joy so sweet is the possibility of sinking into a doomsday or crashing into the chasm between here and the dream, yet landing on the other side in victory. This is why holding the bandera high is so important. It's a beacon of something greater. After all, healthy people don't wade into quagmires chasing after funky depression for a never-ending doomsday. No, we **jump**[5]. Of course, I may stumble into the pit from time to time, but that's only because I've become so set on looking up the trail.

It's not that I'm blind to pits and potholes in the shadows. On the contrary, I'm more aware than ever of the chasm between who I am and who I want to become. Which is why learning to jump all the while shouting "Cannonball!" is such a vital skill. And we're not only jumping over chasms and quagmires, but we're deliberately jumping into risk and adventure and opportunity for greater joy.

Scary? Check.

Resourced? Check.

Game plan? Check.

Bandera of dreams? Check.

Motivation? Check.

Joy? Jump.

I have no idea what Van Halen's song "Jump" is all about. It starts out like a generic "Buck up, kid" message but then shifts into a spastic, "Baby, ow, oh, take a chance on me. Wait, who said that?" spandexy, full-body heave. Whatever the case—and I love this about art—the song is inspiring in that eighties "Gonna win the big game, Coach!" way. So I make it my own. I absorb the big-hair energy of "Jump" into my bloodstream, step up to the edge of the chasm, don my bodysuit, and then I, well, I jump.

"Dive in!" That's what my kids hear in the face of a jump-worthy scenario. Just dive in if you want to see how solar energy works. Dive in if you want to learn how to ride like Danny MacAskill. Dive in if you want to develop real and lasting friendships. Just dive in.

Go ahead and jump.

Let me point out that, in most cases, jumping in doesn't demand a blindfold. Leaps of faith don't demand closed eyes and empty brains. In fact, the bigger the jump, the more worthwhile the research, the awareness of opportunities, and a view of as many of the obstacles as possible. Let's be honest, diving in with more joy and less fear often happens with confidence, and confidence is often born with a clear image of the end goal, a deepening trust in Creator God's faithfulness, and an honest assessment of our own abilities on the edge of the chasm.

After all, we're called to count the cost when it comes to the most important decision of our lives, aren't we?[6] You'd be a fool to put on a blindfold, empty the money from the old mason jar, and begin taking stock. Jesus isn't interested in blind sheep. He wants us to be fully aware of the cross, the tomb and the empty burial cloth. That's a leap of faith.

When my kids sprint across roasting sand toward the Atlantic, they like to know how deep the water is before they get there. They also like to know how the surf is rolling and if there are sharks thrashing about the shoreline in a bloody mess. These little factors help determine technique and timing. They set expectations. Of course, even with a little planning and experience, rogue waves can destroy a perfectly good body surfing rhythm. And yeah, there are times when my kids sprint toward the blue with no plan at all, just a joy-filled, fear-coated, dream-waving, motivated leap from car to crashing waves. I'm sure you're aware that this contradicts my previous note on preparation, but you and I both know that sometimes, clarity or not, we just need to make a splash on the scene.

Without a doubt, the healthier our mindset before the jump, the more legendary the joy. So what do you think? Want to join me in doing a little recon, pressing into Christ for wisdom and squeezing into that old Roth-esque spandex bodysuit for a joy-filled jump?

Joy is at hand. Can you sense it?

K

Kindly Killjoy

Kindness[1] is one of those subtle attributes that shines brighter the longer it's on display. Yet it doesn't really stand out in Paul's famous list of fruits[2], right? Buried beneath joy and hiding in the shadow of self-control—I seem to be endlessly focused on self-control—kindness sits like a mossy stone.

Until recently, I lumped kindness in with goodness and politeness and all those friendly sort-of ailments without giving it much room to breathe. But kindness carries a light of its own. Of course it's rooted in Christ alongside all the other fruits, but in a very humble way it offers something deeper, brighter in the end.

It's precisely the opposite of a killjoy. It's a soul-deep state of being. Well beyond the car salesman–esque smile and past the sweetly rushed handshake on a Sunday morning, kindness is a grace that permeates the fog of another. It sympathizes with an honest response while sacrificing the socially slick win of a snarky reply or an envious bite. Kindness moves at a steady pace, warming, illuminating, drawing others into its orbit like the sun does the earth.

I've seen it. I've felt it.

In Dr. Arnold, my fifth grade teacher who looked a little deeper, reached a little further, and invited us kids in to experience a more exciting version of a school day, genuinely believing we were capable.

In a short-seasoned friendship in Hollywood that cracked open my first taste of intentional discipleship through an Acts-style fellowship.

And in that missional community in Stoughton that shared in babysitting for date nights, served meals at a local shelter, and fostered intentional Bible study for community discussion.

These people and seasons shared traits inherent in the type of kindness Paul notes—a kindness sourced in the Holy Spirit, planted in the soul and grown through trial and togetherness. It's almost as though kindness has been designed to be expressed among others, as if it's meant to be shared. Ever notice how much of the movement of God happens in groups and cords of two, three, or more?

The fruit of the Spirit seem to grow in unison. Joy and self-control intertwine like vines on a trellis. And as Paul describes it, "when the kindness and love of God our Savior appeared, He saved us...because of His mercy"[3]—kindness, love and mercy, united on mission. Not to mention that wherever two or more gather in Jesus's name for His purpose He dwells in grace and truth.[4]

Kindness, like faith, is meant to be spread, but it's also meant to be experienced within our very own bodies through the emotions, attitudes and abilities He breathed into us at birth. And kindness, like other fruit, seems to work best supernaturally from the outside in (God to me) and then from the inside out (me to others).

/ / /

I haven't always been good at being kind to myself, loving my bones with the same grace and truth that sent Christ to the cross for me and my divine being. It's a tricky balance, isn't it? If we're not careful, we might stumble into worshipping our own existence and abilities. I've never been tempted to bow down to my own image, though. It seems to me that self-worship is a bit like deifying homemade sausages. When you know what's behind the scenes, no matter how delicious, you know it's not something to glorify. No, I've tended to lean more into the darker valley of self-depreciation. You know what I mean.

Ever spend time with a **killjoy**[5]? Sure you have. Killjoys have the effect opposite of kindness. Instead of drawing you in to feel the warmth of their light, they propel you outward beyond the great spiral of the galaxy. It's uncomfortable to be around someone who seemingly goes out of their way to let you know that the new car you just bought is actually number two on the list of worst cars ever made. Or that the story you just wrote would probably flow better if you overhauled the main character and the plot. Or that the meal was great but too much salt is the signature of an unskilled chef.

Killjoys are a dime a dozen. Seriously, we're everywhere. It's easy to be one too. I'm a recovering killjoy. Everyday I look for my bandera of dreams, shake off the victimhood, tone down the melancholic critic in my gully and attempt to step out with kindness. It's a struggle, though becoming less and less so every day.

Here's a little secret about killjoys: we don't like being around ourselves either.

What's interesting about shaking off the kill from the joy is that kindness is kryptonite to this character disorder. For instance, if a killjoy were to say, "Rich, I like your book. You'd probably be a notable author if you told stories like Anne Lamott or Roald Dahl," my natural response in my most fleshy-fleshiness would be a sharp comeback or a quiet groan and a swift exit. But that sort of response is full of empty calories. Satisfying for a second, but not fulfilling.

At my best, I'd prefer the gentle, "Those are great authors. Really love Bird by Bird and The Twits. Thanks for reading my book. So I hear you've just earned a raise. Nice job. How'd that come about?" The killjoy might not be immediately aware of what's taking place, the turning over of the downer to reveal a bit of sunlight, but that kindness kryptonite has a way of pressing in and impacting the soul through osmosis. Not to mention it just feels better to steer away from biting remarks. To walk away with my joy still intact.

We can't control another's mindset, but we can set them up for aha moments. We can stand firm, watching with hopeful curiosity as they slowly put the doomsday knife down and instead pick up a bandera of dreams.

/ / /

When was the last time you sat on the front porch, bright blue sky all around, with the simple goal of observing the beautiful forms before your eyes? I haven't used a **kaleidoscope**[6] in years. But, if any art form is both intentional in design yet random in display, it's a kaleidoscope.

The Scottish inventor, David Brewster, stumbled across the exact symmetry of shapes through reflections at particular angles, which launched a series of experiments. His work was soon patented as a kaleidoscope. No, *kaleidoscope* isn't Scottish for "wonderful haggis of the eye." Instead, Brewster fused a few Greek words together to describe his discoveries:

kalos – beautiful

eidos – to see forms

skopeo – to look

Observing beautiful forms.

Seems a bit tame these days, right? A tube full of glass pellets bouncing around mirrors in the light. My screensaver does that just to kill time. I'm not going to try to sell you on the refreshing vitality of spending time with a kaleidoscope, but the practice of observing the beautiful forms around us is something we should all adopt. Why? Because kindness functions like a kaleidoscope.

Kindness, in my experience, is intentional in design yet often random in display. I mean that I have to choose to be kind from my first breath in the morning to my last. At first it was difficult to drop the doomsday knife, but with time and intentionality, it's become easier to pick up the yoke of kindness.

But kindness is also random. I don't know on any given day to whom and in what form kindness will manifest. Of course, my wife and kids will be on the frontlines of this daily experiment, but beyond that, kindness shifts and morphs and rotates and reflects in a million different ways and circumstances.

It's a beautiful thing to observe kindness take shape in its many forms. Do this long enough and we become that living legend, that chronically kind coworker, that walking source of freedom encouraging others to grasp their banderas with grace and truth. Kindness may not move the parameters set in stone for my shy personality, but kindness doesn't shy away from opening heart, mind, soul and body to those random opportunities to be kind, even to a killjoy, like me.

Kindness and killjoys have something in common: they're both infectious. They spread to those they're around, and the more time we spend with them, the more infectious they are. Who are the killjoys infecting you right now? How will you kryptonite the kill before it robs you of the joy set before you? I suppose that's where kindness shines brightest.

L

Living Legend

Have you ever been **lampooned**[1]? No, not harpooned. The latter is the act of being impaled by a large fishing spear. The former just feels like it.

If you're breathing, you've been on the sharp end of a personal spear. Sometimes we earn a shot of sarcasm, like the time you bought that collector's edition triple vinyl pressing complete with t-shirt, latex gloves and dog biscuits instead of paying the rent. Other times, the spear aims for the heart, like when your idea wasn't simply shot down at the team meeting but soon became the encyclopedic example of a foolish thought: "Dude, you pulled a Dyson out there!"

Strangely, there are times when it's funny to be lampooned by someone else, like a good friend. Painfully funny. Like when we take a harpoon to our character and it spills our flaws all over the carpet in a Captain Obvious sort of way. Good friends pull folly into the light with character harpoons for our survival, which is why grace is woven into these tight-knit bonds. Let's be honest: these jabs are inevitable. They're part of growth and discovery. But when we're living a lampoonable rhythm of life, it's time to take stock. Time to evaluate our interest quotient. Time to kick discernment into high gear, observe what makes us tick and consider stitching together a new bandera.

It's not uncommon to lampoon ourselves too. In fact, if you're anything like me, you've made an art form of it. That sort of self-deprecation is funny when breaking the ice on stage but a bit sad and off-putting when it happens at every family party.

Lampooning ourselves is an interesting practice, isn't it? I doubt dogs do this. Or dolphins. Dolphins are too smart to waste time spearing themselves, grinding up their emotions like tuna fish. Yet, for humans, it seems to come naturally. Why do we do this? I haven't met anyone deliberately chasing after a *National Lampoon's* Clark Griswold lifestyle, the embodiment of a bumbling suburban dad. It's a wildly funny satire, but not one to emulate, right? Is it possible, though, that we lampoon our lives blindly? Or out of sheer laziness? I wonder if these amount to the same thing: a misdirected life with no vision of what could be and no mission to tread. A life that torches Christmas trees, destroys cars and flirts with affairs. Dolphins don't do that.

I think about the lampoon often. Some days I can actually feel it like a spear in my lower back. Isn't it awkward walking around with a spear in your back? There it is, agitating Brooke and annoying the kids and knocking that framed watercolor painting by great-grandma off the wall and down the stairs.

Am I living lampooned? Maybe, but it's hard to think straight with this sharp pain in my back.

/ / /

I've been reading through some **legendary**[2] stories of Civil War artists. Men who braved some of the most historic battles, captured victorious moments, sketched unexplainable emotions and pressed into the grit with faith and courage. Ever spend time with a living legend? Someone whose reputation far exceeds their presence? Stories about them seem to pour out of the heavens as though their very shadow produces fruit. Tales you feel in your gut and come away thinking either the stories are exaggerated or these people are mythical creatures reborn.

The funny thing about most of the legends we're aware of, though? They're history. We almost never see them in real time. Maybe a heroine or sacrificial deed or an unexplainable act of kindness, but a legend? No, that's for the future to decide, right?

Legends are stories handed down, gathered by followers and witnesses and generations compiling and repeating. This is what's so amazing about a living legend. The stories are tangible, quickly gathered and virally spread. Your neighbor, the World War II hero. That mom at your kid's school pouring out Christ's love through winter hats and gloves even though her own kids have long graduated. That friend reclaiming the community through his orbit of kindness. Living legends.

I know some of these people. I've met them. I've seen them in action. They often ask, not with words or hints, but with an honest mission and a clear bandera, "Rich, are you living lampooned or living a legend?" You know what's scary about the difference between the two? It's that whatever my course in life, I'll be passing it on to my kids.

Which spills over into our **legacy**[3].

Standing right where you are, on the carpet or in the dirt, what will you pass on to your kids? To those in your circle? To your friends, fans, partners, small group? If nothing changes from this season onward, what will you be sending them into the world with, philosophically, spiritually, financially, materially, relationally, emotionally and so on?

These are monumental questions, right? It's easy to throw up shields with questions like that. To summon the best of our verbal defenses. To involuntarily contort our bodies to speak a language we all understand and want to run from. But I'm tired of shields and defenses. I don't want to perform the emotional contortionist routine again. I want to build a home, not a decrepit circus full of unstable clowns.

To be fair, my kids are more like fire-eaters than morbid clowns. Elias can shake off an emotional burn, forgive in discussion, then dive back in with awesome speed. Ada has a bit more tender flesh on the surface. A sharp word cuts fast and deep. I've teared up alongside her at the sight of my hurtful handiwork on more than one occasion. But a quick apology, some gracious words breathed into her soul, and a long hug and she's a willing player once more.

A tattered circus doesn't offer a legacy of healing and helping. Unstable clowns aren't raised, they're tossed into the ring without a legendary guide.

Yeah, I'm tired of the defenses. Besides, they don't seem to shield me from my own thoughts. And those are the longest battles, the longest nights.

More and more I'm growing confident in the spiritual legacy I'm building beyond the tattered tent. Here on the streets and along the trails, I'm convinced this divine breath in life is the most important element to pass on. I want my kids and their kids and their kids to breathe in and out in their own time. To be personally impacted by the love I have for the Creator who deeply loves them.

Did you know that God is love?[4] That Jesus and the Father are one,[5] and we are in Jesus and He is in us?[6] This Creator God, who is the very embodiment of **love**[7], is the source of my preferred legacy. He's the very same source of Joanna's joy and Ada's adventurous attitude on the bars. The root of Elias's grace to forgive and power to body surf those waves.

This love is both selfless and selfish. In marriage it's worthy of a giant celebration with gowns and salmon-colored tuxedo trimmings, unnecessarily large cakes and circus-sized tents. It holds Brooke in such high esteem that everything from her desired boots to her vital quiet time is worth sacrificing my own shoes and schedules for. Yet this proclaimed love, publicly woven through gardens and parties and date nights, is also deeply private. It winds behind the underwear basket in the closet, glides across the jewelry box on the bookshelf and weaves through softly spoken prayers under covers in the bed—a bed I selfishly share with her alone.

This legacy of love sets boundaries, doesn't it? Boundaries defined and invited into. After all, "This is how we know what love is, Rich: Christ laid down His life for us. And, dude, you ought to continue to lay down your life, your daily rhythm and expectations, for your wife, and your kids and..."[8] It seems to me that the boundaries defined by God's loving sacrifice offer more freedom than the open borders of any "free love" movement.

/ / /

Am I living my desired legacy? Since embarking on this adventure of a lexicon, I've been asking the question daily. My answer? More and more. If my legacy is simply the overflow of a godly rhythm lived in the flesh as I venture toward the manifestation of that hope-filled bandera, then living lampooned isn't all that inevitable. At least not of my own continual doing. Instead, I just live the life I want to live, which happens to be a legacy worth passing down. No clowns. No harpoons. Just love in action.

Have you lampooned your legacy? It's not too late to regroup. People love a comeback story. Redemption is what makes popcorn worth buying at a theater, isn't it? And yeah, the extra butter too.

Are you living lampooned or living a legend?

M

Mindset on Mission

What if you only had three months to live from the moment you read this? Imagine, three months from now you're taking the inevitable dirt nap. What would you want the world to know? What single, unified and personal message would you offer those around you before the gerbera daisies start rising?

It's a simple question.

It's an honest question.

If you're like me, it's a halting question.

Where did your mind race to? What note caused your heart to skip a beat? What turned your stomach a bit? Too many questions, I know. It's unfair. But I'm serious. It may or may not be a hypothetical scenario. Right now I'm sitting on my front porch and it's raining. Actually, it's storming. Lightning, thunder, rain, cool breeze on an 85-degree day. One rogue lightning bolt and I'm powder. What's your message?

I'm bent on playing the victim. Have I mentioned this before? When something doesn't go according to plan, my mind skips the current track and goes straight for the downer ballad at the end of side one. It's an awful mindset to have. We all have one, a rhythmically grooved mindset, and mine has been coasting on melancholy as long as I have memories to show for it. At my weakest, I'm inclined to moan,

"Why me?"

"What's the deal with money. Can't we just barter? I guess I'd have to find a skill first."

"Why am I the one to suffer three flat tires in a week?"

At any given moment, my internal Ricky D. entertains doomsday. Yet when the fog lifts and I can breathe free, I'm able to plant my feet in the soil, drop the needle on track one and reach for the joy tucked in between flat tires. Like a hipster doing manual labor, my responses can be a complex mess.

Mindset[1] is that internal attitude we're prone to engage and reveal. Catch that? It doesn't stay internal for long. The attitude of our mind oozes out of every crack and pore in our body until we've showered everyone who happens to be within crying distance. Just between you and me, I may have a little experience with this. Ask my wife, she probably has a rain poncho you can borrow.

I was soaking in a line from one of Paul's letters, "Your attitude should be the same as Christ's,"[2] when it occurred to me how intricately attitude and mindset are woven together. I had always thought of attitude as an outward display of emotion or the ability to put on a certain face for an audience or a crowd. Then I began to wonder what it would be like to have an attitude like Jesus's. There had to be a depth to attitude, something beneath the skin. Did Jesus ever have a bad attitude? Did He let His emotion take over and alter His demeanor on a dime? Did He simply act tough around religious leaders, yet express genuine humility among His disciples? I've been meditating on that passage for years. Years! It's safe to say that Jesus didn't put on an emotional show for anyone. Ever. He was honest, spirit to bone.

Years ago while reading a commentary for a class on Paul's letter to the Philippians, I was captivated by the author's swap of **attitude**[3] with the word mindset in its place. "Your mindset should be the same mindset as Christ's." Let's put a little more meat on that simple charge: "Rich, your mindset, your internal attitude about everything life has to offer—yeah, that's right, everything—your inclinations should be just like Christ's while He was here traversing the soil. Oh yeah, and your internal readiness ought to spill over onto Elias, Ada and Joanna. The overflow of your mindset throughout your entire being ought to lift up Brooke through muck and majesty. Always." Woven together, right?

Do you think Jesus played the victim card when powerful leaders denounced and planned to execute Him?

I wonder how His heart shifted as His brothers doubted His role in eternity.

What went through His mind as His students, after years of witnessing miracles and absorbing His teaching, abandoned Him?

I don't get the sense that Jesus played the victim internally or externally, only physically. Even then He never lost control. Instead, His focused attitude spilled over onto everyone within spit-in-the-mud-and-rub-it-on-their-eyes distance. Though if anyone was justified in crying foul, He was. He didn't. His heart was tied to greater things. His mindset was singularly positioned to live out the message only He could, even through hoarse whispers on the cross. "Father, forgive them."[4]

/ / /

There's a divine connection between our message and our mindset. Our **message**[5], the one people remember us by, is the overflow of what we value. These values are the accumulation of what we believe about and beyond this life in the dirt, how we spend our money and time and energy, and what gets our ticker ticking—the elements we make decisions by. Values shape our message, and our message echoes around us as we live out our divine mission each and every day.

Ahh, **mission**[6], another great word. The action plan for bringing our message to life. The avenue we choose over and above all others. There are a lot of avenues we might venture down, right? In the past, I've been pressed to decide between making my patch of the world more enjoyable through music OR serving the local church in order to foster discipleship relationships OR partnering with creators to discover their own missions with their own messages. Trial and error, discovery, growth in knowledge and insight, supernatural revelation—these create detours and dead ends, which clarify the road we should take. They've altered my own course for sure.

I'm discovering just how vital it is to have a healthy mindset for handling the daily perils and promises constantly barraging me and my family from all directions. What we value clarifies the message we want to share, and that message, ravaged and refined, over and over and over again, sheds light on the bandera overhead.

When I'm the victim first thing in the morning, the message I desire to share with those around me is swallowed up, digested and disposed of in a pile in the dirt. Just to clarify, there are actual victims out there, but my whining and my moaning are not sourced in bombs, beatings and abuses. No, my victimhood is crouched in the shadows of my own mind, in the doubts and disputes piled high during my stumbles through discernment in faith and truth. My morning fuss is often nothing more than the muck of life we all splash about in.

If I only had three months to live and this book could speak on my behalf, I'd want you to know that you're called to live a God-breathed rhythm of life. I'm convinced more and more and more that Jesus is the source of all that life is and the rhythms, creativity and reasons lived out.

///

If I only had three months left on this planet with the amazing Brooke and our kids and friends and family, well, I suppose I'd wake up and tell that nagging voice of victimhood to simmer down, be still. Actually, I'd probably tell it to go to hell. I'd say it every single day for those ninety days. I'd smile and breath deep and whisper in my kids' ears, "God is love, and love is in you, and you co-create through His love in all you do." I'd ignore the Joneses, whoever they are, and feel sexy in my own skin, beard and all. I'd lead divine adventures with my kids and love my wife with light and insight until those daisies start growing fast and strong. And I'd give credit to Creator Christ for life, no matter how brief, and His grace, no matter how subtle.

Who knows, I may only have a few more breaths beyond this sentence. I suppose it's time to go whisper.

How about you? Maybe three months doesn't quite do it for you. How about three years? How about thirty? Thirty years from now, who do you want to be? What stories do you want to be telling your grandkids? What failures do you want to have overcome, redeemed for the next generation?

You have a message.

N

Nexus of Nobility

Before I set out on this word mission, a curiously confident freedom to say "**No!**"[1] kicked into gear. Now, I had begun to say no to uninspired opportunities and abrasive expectations years ago, but often with a heavy wash of guilt. This new season of saying no, however, has been surprisingly void of that inappropriate sludge.

Something was different with this no that the former no didn't possess. This new no was being sourced from deep inside my gully, the overflow of engaged and approved values. Sounds a bit corporate, I know, but these values, the building blocks of a renewed vision for my future, were not only ushering me forward on my journey but shaping my attitude as well. I was no longer muttering, "No, no, no," curled up in the fetal position beneath the lower rack of my son's closet—which, by the way, sounds like a great opening scene of a novel. Instead, a calm, shoulders-back "No thanks" began to emanate. The advent of another color of confident discernment.

Confidence in God's design for my future.

Confidence in my personal, unique, sexy and divine Rich-ness.

Confidence in the seeds of knowledge planted, the skills tended and the adventures harvested.

"Rich. You. Yes you. You are God's workmanship—a supernaturally unique and vital part of the body of believers worldwide."[2] It's what I tell my kids and what you tell yours. You are designed with something to offer your family, friends and tribe. Find it. Grab hold of it. Say no and shake off the unnecessaries, because at the end of the day, like a dog frozen between a command and the fresh steak on the table, we can't "serve two masters."[3] Maybe we can pull it off for a hot minute, but a fulfilling lifetime? Nope.

Just say no.

No to attempting to live another's dream for our life.

No to good opportunities in order to squeeze the great ones like our kid's favorite Pillow Pet.

No to letting our kids enlist in sixth-grade dating because, well, it's not actually dating, right?

And you know what? Even the mysterious no to my personal desires in sacrifice for others' needs has become more fulfilling. But it's wild how much practice it takes to say no and to say it without anxious convulsions or foaming at the mouth. It's an art form like most other skills and habits. Practice. We make a plan, a simple one, and stick with it until it becomes natural.

"Rich, looks like we're gonna need to stay late again to really pull this off. You in?"

"Not tonight, Hurley."

"I see you've signed up for the standard plan. But for only a couple more bucks a month you could have access to an entire universe of free data and endless content."

"No thanks."

"Dad, I know you said it's time to go, but just another half hour, please? Everyone else will be on all night anyhow!"

"Time's up."

We say no, release the guilt like a scapegoat and allow a little slack into our lives for the next round of opportunities.

Ever been to the beach? I've stood on all four contiguous US coasts, and each one offers something mysteriously familiar. It was on Corolla Beach, NC with that raw saltwater rub between the thighs when this notion came to a head. It struck me how the same eternal catalyst behind the first rolling wave was there within me, eager to carry me on fresh cresting waves into a new mission. But there was one catch: I had to start saying no to all the waves vying for a good ride along the way.

"Pick a wave and don't look back, to the left or to the right. Just ride it, Rich, until it crashes. Then grab another." The ocean has a way of propelling us forward while washing away the muck for a clear view, doesn't it? And yet, guilt has its own way of creeping in like snack lust on a diet. Guilt bottlenecks the flow of the current wave. "Look at that wave, Rich. That wave is faster and smoother and taller. You should be on that wave, don't you think?" By then I'm already choking on the salty brine with one eye closed and falling from the crest.

If you're a waffler, like me, saying no will take a little more energy. A few more rounds of your best late-night DJ voice in the bathroom mirror saying, "No. That's not my wave." Without a doubt, you and I, pure-bread wafflers, need to weave a confident no into our personal lexicon before having our act together. Let's be honest, you probably won't get your act together until your "No, but thanks for the offer" is in full swing and without excuse.

It takes a few rides and a come-to-Jesus moment in that space between wave and sand to catch our bearings.

/ / /

Ever think about the role no plays at the **nexus**[4] of our daily decisions? Great and small, temporal and eternal, mental and physical, we move through a million nexus points a day. Most of them come and go with little fanfare, like the spread I'll put on my sandwich during lunch. Jam or mayonnaise? Not quite life-or-death, I know. And thank God most of our decisions are free from doom. But let's be clear, mayo with fresh apricot jam spread over a toasted baguette, tied together with freshly sliced honey-glazed ham, crunchy romaine and fresh kale from the garden? Life-giving. That's a nexus worth biting into.

Once in a while, however, we hit a vital crossroads. A nexus like no other. That lull between two incredible waves. My decision to marry Brooke was both easy and one of the most complex nexus points I've ever had to process. It demanded a seemingly endless number of noes to both real and imagined what-ifs, yet it required only one audacious "Yes!" to seal the deal now symbolized in the subtle shimmer on her finger. That series of noes entangled in a myriad of nexuses has impacted every decision since, including my wholesale adoption of the apricot jam Brooke introduced me to. That weighty crossroads, which could have been met with a "No, I'm not ready to be done slothin' it on the couch, sporting a Boba Fett helmet and eating day-old Dominos everyday for breakfast," has actually fostered the most beautiful and rewarding relationship I've ever experienced. You know what that means, don't you? Every potentially intimate, flirtatious relationship from that nexus on is a "No, I'm spectacularly taken!" And this immovable no continues to enhance that grand yes spoken all those nexuses ago.

Catch that? Really solid noes, discerned well and boldly acted on, create awesome yeses later on.

It was after my first year of college, through a nexus of relationships, when I connected with that summer camp outside of Mad City to work as a camp counselor for a few months. Ever been to camp? I hadn't.

I had absolutely no idea what I was getting myself into. I didn't even know it was a paid position until I was asked to decide between cash, check or direct deposit. That's either a testament to careless financial planning or a spiritual statement about my values. Or both. Either way, it was a life-changing season.

Spending a summer with a group of like-minded young pseudo-adults on a singular Christ-centered mission was both challenging and enlightening. It became a nexus for values, mission and visions to come.

I've spent a lot of summer days at camp since then, with friends and Brooke and my kids. I've served with incredibly healthy teams, motivated and maneuverable—teams full of advents that uncovered and constructed character, that unashamedly offered their best ideas, that stumbled to their bunks in the dark, and that woke up exhausted in faith yet refreshed through action. Together we fostered copious amounts of fun, both on call and behind the scenes. We shared a divine lexicon. We prayed, knees and elbows and foreheads in the dirt. And when we went to battle, it was for one another.

Ever been with a team like this? You'd remember. Belonging to a healthy team is like donning joy like a Snuggie. It feels like a welcome hug and a hot coffee on a cold and lonely night.

As for teams that missed the mark? Well, we never quite made it beyond the front door. Too many noes at all the wrong nexuses.

And yeah, I've led both of these kinds of teams. I've been at the nexus of each set of character accoutrements. I've worn all the hallmark attitudes with as much glitz as Rush's 1970s robe phase. My time back on Corolla Beach not only instigated a future of healthy noes, but it also began a journey of honest reflection on the noes of past nexuses. Good or bad. In faith or in funk. Humble or hard-hearted. And it changes things. A fresh perspective on past events changes future nexuses.

It changes paths.

It changes teams.

It changes hearts.

/ / /

"Rich, you can't serve two masters. No, you're no exception to this reality." No to the wandering musician dream is a yes to a deeper service. No to the value of a large property in the countryside is a yes to the joy of walking all over town in community. No to watching Netflix every night is a yes to reading this Lexicon. Just say no.

What nexuses are you preparing your noes for? Practice small and be sure to keep an eye on the horizon for the bigger waves as they come.

O

Onymous Others

Following the dissent of Babel, peculiar and diverse bands of **others**[1] formed and dispersed. Carrying the message of God and attempting to connect, or maybe disconnect, its meaning, they wandered into new places, settling and saturating their new land. New habits, beliefs, and rituals sprang to life.

It was in that otherness, that movement beyond Babel, when the Creator personally invited an original unknown on an adventure: "Abram from Ur, leave your land, tribe and family homestead and I will build you into a great nation. I will bless you. You and Sarai will be blessed and become a blessing among all the others in the land."[2] Does that qualify as an aha? Or is it more of a "What the...?"

This call from God to an other, a man belonging to a tribe far removed from the message of Babel, sparks my soul a bit. If you've survived middle school you know what I mean. Others are easy to spot. We're distinct. Separate. Not from around here. Not of the collective mindset. Others are a notch beyond the belt. To see Creator God personally invite this ancient other is refreshing. It reignites my curiosity in this God beyond the struggle.

We know these others too. Maybe not personally. We weren't around in that age between Babel and Abram, but I think we all know some others like them in our own walk and way. Others just beyond the circle we're currently in.

The quiet one with a notebook and giant pack of artsy pencils who doesn't talk much.

The sports nut obsessed with the Steelers, alone and weeping into a small towel.

The agnostic who clearly doesn't believe in or show interest in the God I know.

Maybe you're the other.

Maybe your husband's an other. I know he's rad, God knows he is, but the gaggle in your network hasn't caught on yet, right?

Maybe your daughter is. Of course she's talented and bright and beautiful. I agree. And one day she'll run with a tribe who understands her.

When we lean into Abram's ancient story, we're actually pressing in on something personal. We're leaning into the advent of a divine invitation to all the others looking for a tribe. An invitation we desire. An invitation we pray our kids will experience from the right circle with the right soul. But it's also an invitation to be passed through and offered by us. We invite the Abrams into our own adventure. Our tribe. Our mission. And we rest in the hope that otherness isn't really what we think it is.

/ / /

If you think about it, the other isn't all that mysterious. Some are, I guess. Some are creepy, like the kinds of others we train our kids to discern, refuse the candy and run from. Most of the time, though, I think others are simply kindred versions of you and me and our kids.

Something internal shifts when we see these others in the way that Creator God saw that man from that other tribe from beyond the river. Doomsday dissipates. Discernment settles in as hope spills outward.

I spent a season with a guy who had this innate ability to belittle the other. It was a honed skill, sharp and swift, like the strike of a professional bowhunter. Impressive, really. A person had a different vocation than his own? A different dialect? A hairstyle unbefitting of his bubble? A shirt a bit too quirky? Line up in sight, steady breath, denigrating broadhead launched straight to the heart. Often, it took little more than a slight crack in their voice for this guy to begin mentally field dressing their wounded, other-like soul.

"Dude, ever notice your tolerance for the differences of others only extends as far as your arm?" I said.

"Nah. But even if I am a little biased, I pretty well hit the mark on my observations. The right kind of different, you know?"

No. I didn't know. Not his version of different, anyhow. I've been an other. I still am in most circles. I'm a strange guy. Awkward. And while I'm not always discerning, I can imagine Abram and Sarai, God's kind of different, standing among the others.

I have another friend who genuinely honors the other. He told me about a group of seniors he was driving around town. Telling a story in the van, one of the seniors stuttered, stumbled over her words in excitement, and that was all it took. The rest of the group pounced. Mock stuttering. Laughing. Tearing and gnashing. Not a sliver of grace among them.

"So how did she respond?" I asked.

"She stopped talking. Wouldn't you?"

Killjoy had arrived. Her smile faded. The joy of reminiscing squelched. Proof that we're never too old to feel the sting of humiliation from the other side of the social divide. My friend watched the woman's eighty-five-year-old frame shrink at the verbal onslaught.

"How did you follow up?"

"I challenged them to grow up and then invited them to apologize when they felt the sting of healthy rebuke."

I think Jesus did that, didn't He? "Step forward if you're free from sin. Step forward and throw the first stone of condemnation and death at this woman if you're entirely guiltless yourself."[3]

Jesus steps in with a divine defense of the other. But He also reaches out with an invitation for you and I to understand their otherness. He pushes back on the divisive. That's what my friend did in that van. He pushed back on the mob in order to offer freedom to the other. He lives this way too. He lives that legend. He pushes back stereotypes and leans in to grasp cultural, spiritual, and familial expressions different than his own. There's a divine curiosity in that type of life, isn't there?

/ / /

One aspect that's so inviting about the story and character of Christ is that His otherness is **omnidimensional**[4]. In all directions and throughout all points on the compass He universally engages humanity with His open invitation to know Him and His justice and His grace and His truth. I can't help but see Jesus as the ultimate bridge across the river of otherness. The bridge over the raging waters of change as my kids grow into their own skin with their own voices and purposes. The bridge between Brooke and me when my otherly qualities push me beyond the bounds of normalcy. He's even the bridge connecting you and me when we cross paths at the grocery store as we reach for different kinds of beer and salsa and chips.

Christ's omnidimensional reality plays a kaleidoscopic role under the roof of my house. I think Paul had this in mind when he wrote to the Ephesians: "I pray that you, being rooted and grounded in love, may have power, united with all the saints, to grasp how wide and long and high and deep this love of Christ truly is."[5] This two-thousand-year-old prayer for a group of others now long gone? Well, it's active and engaged in my home.

Crossing these bridges side by side, there are days when my family strains to grasp the depth of Christ's approachable love. Other days we seem to nestle into it like a family-size bean bag chair. Paul's description of God's omnidimensional otherness is a mind-blowing picture of how Christlikeness can be both mysterious yet familiar. Immeasurable yet traversable. Gracious yet demanding. It's a parental view of life, isn't it?

Do your kids have ideas? Like, dozens of ideas? Per day? My kids have a million. They have ideas about their future vocations, and inventions waiting to come to life, or adventures that need to unfold ASAP, about parties that would be hopping, and games that haven't been created yet, or foods that would taste great if applesauce were involved, and about ways God could reveal Himself to us on a hike in the middle of the forest. An endless multitude of ideas. As their dad, I have the honor of nurturing these lightning strikes. I get to foster space and time and curiosity, omnidimensional elements of discovery. I get to speak both the gritty reality, "You're not quite ready for that yet," all the while saying, "You'll never be ready if you don't practice and discover and research and fail and get back up." Multi-directional love through guidance.

Encourage yet reign in.

Challenge and invite.

Chisel off the rough edges, then polish the talents and abilities and divine gifts.

Prepare for doomsday while helping build bridges to all those others.

I'm convinced more and more that Jesus is the ultimate Other at the nexus of all omnidimensional movement.

And by the way, it's impossible to connect with the others—I mean truly build that living and breathing bridge to those mysterious tribes—without choosing to be **onymous**[6], named and known. Because being an open invitation for something better demands that we stamp our name on our omnidimensional movement, our ideas, our faith, our creation, our kids.

Names are intimate. Naming someone shows value. It's a piece of what sets us apart from all the crawling, swimming and flying creatures around us. We name our kids the way God named Adam, the first man, made in His image and fully aware of his own name and value.

Remember what Forrest Gump did before striking the motherload of shrimp? He named his boat, and even seemed to have the perfect name on hand when the time came. Claiming a name is key for distinguishing one from another. Our names are essential if we're going to settle into our skin. And it's impossible to express divine otherness of God without one.

"What should I call you? Who should I tell them sent me?"

"Tell them I am who I am. Tell them YHVH is sending you."[7]

YHVH clearly stated who He was and still is. Mysterious? Sure. Clear in name? Yep. Why? Because names invite us in. Moses wasn't responding to some god in the panoply of gods. He was responding to The God. The God that is beyond and above all other ideas and images about God. "I am The God. That's what you can call me."

Healthy movements travel behind healthy leaders. And healthy leaders are approachable. They're known. Which means that finding the others isn't a one-way pursuit. Finding others requires that we allow ourselves to be found—think Moses at the burning bush. To be available—think the Twelve's response to Jesus's calling. To throw ourselves out there unashamed of our bandera of dreams and missional movement—think Paul's letter to Philemon. We sign our work with our values, releasing that unhealthy pull to remain anonymous.

We all desire to know and be known. I do. And I have the singular honor of calling Elias and Ada and Joanna my kids. Naming them and then calling them by name.

We're co-creators. Partners in our adventures on purpose. We know our partners. We trust them. We engage our audience and our friends and our family intentionally, revealing those things others aren't willing to set on the public altar.

Living endlessly engaged is most enjoyable when we're engaged authentically with others. This is the stuff legends are made. Living omnidimensional lives in pursuit of a grand vision flying high above the fray, surpassing the killjoys on doomsday while jumping in feet first, ready to create and connect with all the others.

P

Purpose

Do you remember the first time you joined the ancient chorus, asking, "Why am I here?" Not here reading this lexicon, but here in the dirt, here in the flesh. I was in middle school when this idea of purpose, life purpose, crept into my mind and pricked my soul. **Purpose**[1], design, reason for being and having and doing.

I don't know about you, but it's only now, in my middling age, with the light of hindsight streaming in through the trees, that I'm able to see past decisions in greater detail. I'm more aware that purpose was hiding in the shadows all along. It's an awesome privilege to catch a glimpse of the movement of a God who is for me and with me and beyond my understanding.

Like when the doctor told me it was severe tendonitis and that the only way to truly care for it was to quit playing the bass guitar, which meant dropping out of school, which felt like failure. "Why? Why me? What's the actual purpose of life then?" A guttural question from the pit. Of course I hadn't failed. It's not as though I had any control over the assailing -itis, and I still don't, but the loss was suffocating. A dream, an idea of who I was supposed to be, had been eliminated at point-blank range, out of my control and orchestrated within my own body.

Isn't it wild how tendonitis or cancer or a broken relationship can both sink a vision and yet reveal a deeper purpose?

Purpose—the reason for moving toward a particular destination, object or goal. I get the impression that most of us don't meditate all that much on the micro-purposes, those everyday particulars that simply happen. Like making coffee for the purpose of enjoying a warm beverage before the sun rises and rising along with it. Not particularly majestic, I know, but done with purpose nonetheless.

Now, I actually believe it's worth examining these daily habits, like how Brooke and I greet the kids in the morning and how we prepare dinner every night. No matter how small, these micro-purposes fill in the gaps between us and our greater vision. They're meaningful engagements that build a stronger bridge to a better life. I want to greet my kids well in the morning to usher them into a new day full of love and grace. I want to prepare a family-style meal in the evening to both nourish their bodies and build a bond and rhythm. Micro-purposes have depth, don't they?

Yet, when I'm asking that gut-level "Why am I here?" I'm not typically asking about the role of dinnertime habits, though simple questions like this can be a catalyst for deeper insights depending on the chaos of the day. No, "Why am I here?" is often more about pressing into the grand scheme of it all. It's a gut-churning question that attempts to make sense of all the micro-purposes we're committed to. It's about digging below the edifice of the moment for a more solid foundation.

I think I'm finally grasping the simplicity of Jesus's response to those religious scholars and lawyers when asked about the macro-purpose of life: "Love God with every ounce of your being. First and foremost do that. Second, and this is just as vital, love others to the very same degree that you love yourself."[2]

Why do I exist? To love the very same God who created me in His image and continues to love me deeply.

Why am I here? Because loving God and being loved by God spills over into loving myself, the man I'm designed to be.

What's the purpose of my life? Well, that self-love spurs me on to love others with the very same sacrificial love of the Living God.

Rich, when you wake in the morning, grumpy and set in your ways, love the tribe under your roof with the ancient and ever present love of the Living God.

Rich, when you miss the mark and the goalposts topple, make it a point to purposefully offer God's very own love and respect to yourself in and through and beyond the failure.

Rich, as you live and breathe and chase after your bandera, love those around you with a divine purpose that surpasses the water bottle, the loaf of bread and the shirt off your back.

Jesus's response unpacks purpose on a grand scale in a handful of words, doesn't it? After the bass guitar was taken from my withering arms, a fog settled in around me for a while, but when it cleared, I could see, once again, the overarching purpose of life here in the dirt. Love God. Love myself. Love others. Love them more than that guitar and that dream.

Easy? No. Clear and concise and beyond all earthly banderas? No doubt.

"This is the message I've heard from Him and declare to you: God is light. In Him there is no darkness at all."[3] This light of purpose clears the fog. And just as light feeds plants, it feeds our souls. It empowers and emboldens us and shoves off the confusion of darkness.

What darkness? Of course that's a reference to sin, but stop for second from letting your mind go straight to the depravity of murder and cancer and slavery and abuse. I know that light reveals those evils and fosters purpose in the midst, but light also breathes life into the darkness of the mundane. For those of us caught up in providing for our kids and driving to work and shopping and hobbying, darkness impedes our ability to grasp the nature of our divine role. It plays tricks with our eyes and hearts and minds. It causes us to believe that the bass guitar or the dinner menu or the leaking pipe holds greater purpose simply because it's tangible right now in the struggle.

But there's more to our immediate story of struggle, isn't there? Our stories have a more expansive narrative. They have a macro-purpose woven throughout.

/ / /

I have a confession to make. I don't have this entirely figured out. That's obvious, and that's not my confession. I'm figuring it out. I'm in the process of discovering more and more of the wisdom wrapped up in Jesus's God-self-others trifecta of purpose in love. But, I'm embarrassed to say that I still find myself getting **pissed**-off[4] at an off-kilter event. There it is; that's my confession. It's frustrating that while I've grasped this divine purpose, I still get hijacked from time to time.

I know, I know, pissed isn't a word to be used in a Christ-themed book, let alone emboldened and focused on, but it's important to touch on, at least for the melancholies in my tribe.

You would think that coming to terms with the loss of a major dream, the crashing of one wave and the catching of another, would set me up to handle any and every broken micro-goal dooming my daily rhythm. But there are times when even the whisper of a thought of a little rogue wave, like an unexpected house project, turns my stomach a bit. Why does that pipe have to break now? I have breakfast to make. We have showers to take. We have a day to begin. We have work to accomplish and goals to pursue. We have bills to pay and savings accounts and tithes and IRAs. Frustrated by the endless stream of micro-purposes filling every minute of every hour of every day pushed to the edge.

And yet, I can look back five years and see that bitter, purpose-smothering killjoy begin to wean and weaken in the light of grace-filled purpose. Corolla waves offering insight. Ahas cutting through the noise. I can see and feel the slow and steady movement away from flippant frustration and toward patient purpose.

Pissed? Yeah, but less and less.

At a certain point, **perspective**[5] shifts. It has to. Discernment of purpose seeps into the blood, building and encouraging and shifting from lampoon to legacy. This budding ability to see life, all of life, in light of greater purpose and promise is the alternate lens to that of unending pissed-offedness.

I made three trips to the hardware store to repair the most recent hot water line leak in my basement. Three. Three distinct car trips to purchase distinctly incorrect or unforeseen parts. At least it wasn't four, right? To be honest, and I'm not bragging here, this fracture in my daily purposes didn't overwhelm. It didn't tank my week. I had this aha moment in the basement. I could actually feel the subtle, internal perspective shift toward seeing a greater purpose in that flawed pipe. With every trip to the store and back I saw an opportunity to make it better and learn something manly about shut-off valves, PEX, and SharkBites. You know, own the resource so the resource, this water line, wouldn't own me.

For centuries, prophets and teachers and mountaintop leaders longed to grasp the purposes of God beyond the garden and the toil, the wandering and the sacrifices. But it wasn't until Creator Jesus began revealing Himself as Rabbi Jesus in the flesh that this became expansively possible. That now a bald man with broken water lines in Northern Ohio might repair them with "eyes that see and ears that hear."[6]

Eyes that see purpose from a new angle.

Ears that hear truth with depth and insight.

Once light breaks into the loss and hurt and anger, those of us willing are able to see that divine message, both micro and macro, with fresh eyes. The call to love God, self, and others, it's for all of us, yet I'm the only one capable of experiencing my special blend of tribe, spirit, and DNA right here in my home. And you in yours.

/ / /

Why am I here? Well, to feed my kids and to move toward my bandera, but to do these things filled to the brim with Christ's divine love on purpose.

Can you hear it? That steady hum of heaven riding below the packed dirt of the trail on your way toward that bandera of dreams? Whatever your vision is, whatever your mission or goal, divine purpose hums along. It fills quagmires and builds bridges. Do you hear it? Or are you too pissed-off to notice? Purpose may be in the shadows, but it's near.

Q

Quintessential Quagmire

To this day I'm convinced that mewithoutYou's "Catch for Us the Foxes" is the quintessential indie-alt rock album. Released in 2004 with a slew of legendary records to follow, "Foxes" catches me in all the right places. As far as indie rock goes, it's entirely satisfying.

Let me guess, you've never heard of them. You'd rather I talk about Zac Brown Band or Lecrae or that Hillsong album recorded live (that's right, they're all recorded live). The catch is, I don't really know anything about these artists. They don't strike me in the gully, and to be honest, I'm not interested in analogizing an artist that doesn't punch me in the gut.

So here we are, at the feet of the "Foxes." No doubt, musicians and obsessives alike hold differing opinions about it. Some prefer a thrashier guitar tone (though I'm sold). Others kick against the bounding sway of the rhythm section (my head bobs uncontrollably). One or two might even scoff at the perfect blend of spoken word, gentle sing-song and shout 'n scream vocal incantations of the singer and lyricist (I'm all in). That's not the point. In a mysterious way, "Foxes" captures a genre smack-dab in the middle of the pack, winding through melodies and moods while capturing hearts, minds and souls in its gracious clutch. You see, it quintessentially nails the sound, movement, feel and direction of the indie scene in its day. In my day.

Dramatic? Yeah.

True? I think so.

Quintessential[1] is one of those Q words that often gets lost in the mix. I'm sure I've tossed around perfect model or typical and especially ideal. That last one in particular creeps up in place of quintessential more often than it should. Turns out, there's a thin layer of Merriam-Webster separating the two with important distinction.

Ideal sits on the throne as the high and mighty standard within an art form or way of life or belief system. Attainable? Possibly. But more often than not it carries the weight of what should or could be in its most perfect state of existence.

The ideal state.

I don't live in that state. I live in Ohio.

Quintessential, on the other hand, is more of an active embodiment of something within a particular context. It's like buying shoes. I'm not interested in spending hundreds on the ideal pair of shoes for my height, weight and mobile agility. I don't have any tournaments to win, or play in for that matter. But I also don't want a crappy pair of shoes— shoes that roll ankles and treat my lower back the way a wave treats a newbie surfer. I want the quintessential pair in the middle of the heat. Not too hot and not too cold. Like "Foxes" amidst a bunch of post-hardcore, pre-whatever-came-afterward indie albums in its season. The quintessential sound of indie-alt rock was swallowed up, chewed on like cud and digested by mewithoutYou, from A to B.

I wonder if quintessential is really just a hearty image of an ideal but with flesh on, full of imperfection and grace.

/ / /

Through my late twenties I had this notion that others would do well to adopt my image of the ideal. Name the subject and I offered some flavor of Richie's top shelf that others weren't living up to. Yeah, and neither was I. I know, I know, I'm that guy. At least, I was that guy.

Before the advent of this lexicon, the top shelf was overhauled by a new bandera. That old cudgel, weighted with ideals and used to bludgeon others, has since been traded in for pen and notebook. Vague ideals replaced by curiosity about all the whats and hows life has to offer. The value of divine wonder and adventure in place of shoulds and musts. **Questions**[2] offer that outlet of change. The overflow of heartfelt curiosity, questions are part of the rescue plan on the way to a better bandera. And it's saying them out loud, with grace and a willingness to hear another's heart, bear another's burden for a while.

It's hard to shake, though, isn't it? It's similar to an addiction in that way. You know, bludgeoning others with our demanding and demeaning idealism, unaware of own shortcomings, unhealthy and unattractive. I picture all those movie drunks shouting and slurring and then later depressed with that shocked "Did I really say that?" hangover regret. I can still taste the tonic. It sucks thinking back on those moments, seasons and years, doesn't it?

It does make me wonder, though, if chasing after the quintessential is the point. After all, if athletes, even quintessential athletes, chase after anything short of the ideal, well, they're really just chasing after an image. A really good one, no doubt, but an image of the standard that currently is. Is it really worth running a race if the goal is to stay in the middle of the pack?

Which begs the question, who was mewithoutYou chasing after? I don't really know, to be honest. But I imagine the band was inspired by artists they admired and thought the world of. Music that pushed them to create genre-defining music of their own.

I think that's the key. That's why it's so important that our bandera of dreams be a notch or ten beyond our current reality. We may end up living the quintessential life among our family and friends and community, but only by chasing the ideal with questions and not clubs.

No longer sipping my own top shelf, I'm free to be curious, listen deep and speak the lexicon forming at my core. I want to speak it authentically, don't you? And with such humble devotion that a day without these soul-growing words is a sign that something's off.

Perfect? Nope.

Quintessentially Dysonified? Absolutely.

/ / /

That isn't to say I don't get bogged down in the **quagmire**[3] of what-ifs and disappointments now and again. Which is probably why I walk around town with a cane these days. Even so, God's ground is infinitely more stable. His bridges far wider. His top shelf bottled straight out of that throne room river and sipped on my front porch.

It wasn't until my early thirties, puffing a cigar while sipping a rum and Coke beneath the stars, that it sunk in: Creator God doesn't abandon us to those foggy quagmires.

It sounds so simple doesn't it? After all, "I, Jesus, will be with you always"[4] and "It's no longer I who live, but Christ who lives in me"[5] sound like pretty solid commitments to a redeemed people in a foggy world. But there's a difference between knowing something and grasping something.

I remember blowing smoke rings, or at least smoke blobs, and watching those white wisps swirl in the moonlight, thinking, He's not only with me, but He's inviting me into the quintessential Christian life, here and now, in the midst of all the precarious situations and scenarios I stumble into. For a melancholic, that's a hurricane gust of fresh air. The Rescuer I thought I'd been leaning on actually became the Rescuer I thought I'd been leaning on. I just hadn't grabbed hold of Him in all those quagmires. I think I was too busy smoking cigars and reading about Him.

It's mind-blowing that before I even knew what prayer was, Christ, in the stirring of His own quagmire, had already prayed for me. On the night of His arrest, crossing through the city toward that Olive garden, maybe even standing at the foot of the temple, Jesus prayed for you and me, future believers, quintessential God-breathed travelers. "Father, I have given Rich and Brooke the glory that You gave Me, that they may be one as We are one, I in them and You in Me."[6] Not that we would become God, the absolute ideal, but that we would be unified images of Him and with Him.

And what's more, what's worth its weight in divine salt, is that Christ, the Ideal in the dirt, encourages us to live out our uniquely quintessential versions of His divinity how we see fit. But right there's the catch. I'm chasing after Christ the Ideal and in the process becoming Rich the Quintessential. Sure, it's not the most riveting title for a noble character. I don't imagine the history books will be setting aside chapters for Rich the Quintessential. However, if chasing my bandera leads to an adventurous life within a pack of bandera-chasing adventurers, well, I'm cool with the quintessential title.

/ / /

It's hard to pull ourselves from the quagmire with bludgeon in hand, isn't it? But that's just it: Creator Christ sent the Holy Spirit to empower and assist and even carry us onward through both the muck and mystery of our God-breathed travels. We couldn't pull ourselves out of the swamp with two free hands and a jetpack.

We need our divine Partner.

We need Him to take the cudgel from our claws and slip a pen in its place.

We need a better lexicon.

We need Him to inspire a chase for the ideal with a view of the quintessential—a view that shifts the game, frees us to enjoy the show.

How does it feel to shift from ideal killjoy to quintessential hopeful? Totally righteous.

R

Righteous Dude

*R**ighteous**[1]* is one of those words, like *awesome*, that's been transmogrified into slang. Three hundred years ago I might have been burned at the stake for shouting, "Hey, Elias, righteous carve on your board!" down the Ohio Towpath. Righteous? Really? For leaning on some shaped bamboo with wheels. Light the fire.

Follow the word through history and we see, like most words, it wound through varied forms and functions on the way to my lexicon. In this case, two words collide on that journey: *right* and *wise*. At its source, this is a really good word.

Sacrificial living. Stewardship. Humility in leadership.

Longboarding? Nope. Not on the list of divinely inherent righteous activities.

But let's not write boarding off so quickly. After all, curiosity doesn't always kill the cat. Take a look at my son's boarding from another perspective. Father-son time in action. Challenging physical activity beyond his comfort zone. Stretching social experiences and skills. Spiritual discussions side by side in adventure. And in the midst of these longboarding trips, through dedication and risk, he begins to hammer out smooth turns, carving from one side of the path to the other with ease. The right form now wisely executed at the right time. Totally righteous boarding.

Seems to me that righteousness might actually be woven through benign activities like longboarding and basketball and gardening. Why? Because right and wise are divine traits lived out by humans pressing into Christ. And where humans are, God is at work in righteousness. So, while the root of the word doesn't change, we can definitely add another layer of daily practice to it. We can choose to live righteous lives in all of the nooks and crannies of our schedules. Stewards of right and wise living with purpose here on the trail.

I was thinking about Abram the other day and his claim to righteousness. Abram, like most ancient creatures of faith, seemed to engage God with this gritty type of humility and trust. But Abe's something special in the mix. He was drawn out of his tribe, before there was an ancient Israel, before the Holy Land, before the Scriptures were Scriptures. He followed, imperfectly yet singularly chosen. He left Canaan, but on his terms. He married, but pretended to be a bachelor for convenience. He prayed for children, but took matters into his own hands, literally. And when he finally obeyed without fail, forcing his son to carry the tree for his own sacrificial fire on his back, the Lord intervened with a blessing for His chosen one.

His path wasn't smooth. His ability to carve with grace was anything but gracious much of the time. Yet his righteousness wasn't sourced in his actions or his sacrificial decisions or his family line. It stemmed from his belief. Abram believed what God was telling him, "and God counted him righteous for his belief."[2]

Think about that. Abram was dubbed righteous by thought, before any movement or progress or leadership. Of course those imperfectly action-oriented traits overflowed from his belief, but they weren't the source.

In light of the role Abram's belief played in the history of God's tribe, it seems that calling my son righteous for pulling off a smooth move on his board not only falls short of the divine power of the word, but it's also putting too much weight on my son's boarding abilities. There's a heavenly heartbeat behind Abram's righteousness, isn't there? Elias wasn't a righteous boarder because he grew in function and skill on the board. No, he's a righteous boarder because he believed me when I told him that one day he would ride like a pro and then he went out there right by my side and wrapped that belief with action, like bacon around a thick filet.

He rode.

He practiced.

He fell.

He made rash decisions at times.

He grew in feel and trust and ability.

He was a righteous boarder, and it's my job as a dad, made in the image of God the Father, to bless and train and call out the righteousness of my kids.

When this happens, when we're living right and wise in our flesh according to Christ's divine truth and moral character, we're embodying the Abram flavor of righteousness. We're acting on belief and then overflowing with action. Totally righteous.

I guess that's why it's so important to understand this word in our homes and in our relationships. Words mean things, even today. And not every thought and deed can be praised as right and wise. When I invite my kids into God's righteousness, I'm inviting them into an ancient-divine faith in One infinitely more wise and true and right than myself. But I'm also praising more than their skills in STEM and sports and art and

Scripture memory. I'm actually building them up in their core belief about who Designer God is and how He wired them to live out STEM and sports and art and faith.

/ / /

My kids are constantly grappling with the tension between rebellion and reliability. Small acts of rebellion—"Hold on. I've almost beat this level. Just gotta finish this one...last...oh, wait...I think...I'm almost..."—alternate with small decisions that shine reliability—"Hey, Dad, I finished sweeping the living room. Oh, I did the upstairs hall and bathroom too."

My kids are young and their **rebellion**[3] is small in scope. It's the perfect season to watch them wrestle with it, cut it into in bite-size chunks, taste it and then spit it out like poison. I'm aware that I'm mildly delusional to think these kids won't ratchet up rebellion with age and ability. Of course they'll break through some family values like Chris Farley through a coffee table. They'll question and push on ancient boundary stones. They'll question God's provision and possibility. But I'm convinced that learning from the bitter taste of budding rebellion in this elementary season will help formulate a recipe for that sweet sauce of trust, honor and reliability later.

You and I, we have this opportunity to engage the annoying tone, the frustrating repetition, the obnoxiously disobedient outbursts with steadfast grace and repetitious rebuke. Do I enjoy this part of the job? No, not particularly. I'd rather lick sandpaper than discipline my kids, again. But I'd also rather travel with Ada as she learns the risks and ropes of honesty over Halloween candy than over social media, senior finals or resumes.

It's the difference between scuffing knees on a Huffy and crushing bones in a sedan. I don't know about you, but Brooke and I would rather paste on a million Band-Aids while teaching them how to breathe in the Word of God in their youth than work through rehabs and courts and shelters and the ensuing tsunami of regret as they stumble into adulthood. Either way, I'm their dad. I'm in for the long haul.

I guess, overall, we don't mind witnessing their failures and frustrations here and now. Yeah, it breaks my heart to see them struggle and fall, but it's such a short fall at this stage. And while they're down in the shadows, we reach for the low-hanging, righteous super fruit of parenting: discipline, comfort and guidance.

Let's struggle now, together.

Let's paint the picture of healthy adventure and investment.

Let's remind them who they already are in God's kingdom.

Let's find the better road, the narrow road, the road that's more difficult but endlessly hope-filled. Let's do this before money, relationships, profession and ministry are entangling their hearts and minds on the edge of a much higher cliff, a greater fall and a devastating impact.

But the journey isn't really about rebellion, is it?

The anxiety of what troubles *might* overcome them is the mindset of a killjoy. Melancholic parents are prone to wandering into these *mights* and *what-ifs*. I don't want to soak in that poison. It's the same poison injected into our hearts and minds when we soak in the wounds, failures and regrets of the past. What I really want is to swim in the hope of what could be. The kaleidoscopic wonder of what Creator God is doing in their hearts and minds and hands today for a better tomorrow.

I suppose this is why we pray for them, right? Of course it's to avoid the weight of the curse, but even that vital focus misses the infinite beauty of the journey underway. We want our kids to have the healthiest friendships imaginable. To be wildly successful in their apprenticeships. To stand strong in their universities. To know their strengths and weaknesses far beyond our attempts at defining them. We plead with God to grant them long lives, vibrant marriages, healthy kids of their own and faith experienced in the nooks and crannies. But most importantly, we pray that they will have the means to care for us when we're old and shuffling around their kitchens in our well-loved bathrobes looking for coffee and a bagel, all the while humming the *Star Wars* theme at 3:00 a.m. on a Saturday. We pray for these things.

We beg His Spirit to guide and prompt and foster discernment. I do.

Rebellion? For a season. A reliable spirit catching waves of divine movement? I like the sound of that.

/ / /

Reliability[4] is priceless, isn't it? I know, I know, it's possible to be reliably rebellious. If that's your prerogative, there are some great books you can check out. This isn't one of them. As a dad, I have the honored duty of shaping and molding and inviting my kids when their knees are skinned, their hearts are aching and their minds unsure of what's to come. I get to ask the questions that open hidden doors to hidden bunkers of the soul.

"Since we trust the Author of truth, what can we do when we're tempted to lie?"

"How would you do that differently next time?"

"What inspired you to serve beyond your scheduled chores?"

"When we fail at something, what can help us get back up and try again?"

"How did it feel to lie and lose some trust? What's a better option?"

Do you ever freeze at the thought of being the bottleneck to your kids' experience of reliability? That thought sucker-punched me the other night as I was saying, "Maybe. We'll see." Of course, there's nothing inherently wrong with that response. Sometimes we simply need to ease up on the throttle in order to catch a better view of the plan for the day. But that was not this. I could actually feel the lining of my stomach peel back in ulcerous retaliation as I muttered those words...again. "I don't know, guys. Let's just see how things go."

An aha moment for sure.

I hadn't promised anything. I wasn't backing out of a scheduled event. I've participated in dozens of late-night LEGOfests. But I'm also a high-functioning noncommitter. Not an anti-committer. After all, I show up for meals, not to mention I'm faithfully married after many years of joy-filled postnuptials. Yeah, this sounds like a *Seinfeld* episode taking shape. My point is, I'm inclined to be wishy-washy and my noncommittal attitude is a bottleneck to my kids' soul-deep understanding of reliability. That's a big deal.

That's where the aha moment kicked my spiritual ulcer into high gear. "Am I **raising**[5] the bandera of dreams up high for my kids or **razing**[6] their relational hopes into a pile of rebellion?" Okay, maybe I've dramatized the wording a bit. To be honest I don't remember the precise aha thought, but it definitely flowed in that vein.

Every single day I have the opportunity to offer a righteous word in response to my kids. I'm able to offer the reliability of a dad who wants to show up on purpose, raise the banner, and take the hill. But I'm also able to burn it all down with a few lazy words and even lazier actions.

Abram was not a perfect man, just a righteous one. He pressed into a lifetime of reliable faith and following. He raised the banner of life and truth for an entire tribe. Did Abram miss the mark? Yep. Did he continue in belief? Yep.

Sure, my righteous rhythms and beliefs aren't a guarantee that my kids will follow in my wanderings, but it's a hell of a lot better than tossing them to the lying teeth of wolves growling, "Hey, kid, just do what makes you feel good!" Nah. I don't know about you, but I'd rather offer my imperfectly righteous reliability through Creator God's love than any number of the perfectly broken, socially defunct, spiritually bankrupt worldviews offered by anonymous wolves in coyotes' clothing.

Love on them. Disciple them. Coach them. They're entrusted to us, so let's honor and enjoy that divine trust.

/ / /

What do you celebrate in your home? Is it righteous? Actually right and wise, like Christ's character carved out shoulder to shoulder on longboards with your kids? Or do you find yourself coming in like a wrecking ball, razing hope to the ground? Listen, you still have breath in you. right? Wake up tomorrow morning, open your palms, raise your eyes to the hills and ask, "where does my help come?" Know this, "your help "comes from the Lord, the Maker of heaven and earth. He keeps your feet steady on the journey as you raise your kids, grow in reliability and righteously move forward. In the same way that He provided for His chosen tribe, He provides for you in Ohio, or wherever you are, now and always, without fail."[7]

Yeah, God is more reliable than that sun over those hills. Are you ready for a new dawn?

S

Salvaging Serendipity

How many early morning cups of Breakfast Blend have you consumed feeling like the ship has sailed? Like you had your shot and blew it, period, and now you're living in an emotional van down by the river?

My amazing daughter Ada and I were out for a one-on-one. April in Northeast Ohio is a gamble. Flip-flops and fleece. We decided it was time to break winter's grip with a Frosty, a picnic table and a psalm.

With teeth chattering, we read, "The Lord is my shepherd, I lack nothing."

Goose bumps rising, "He makes me lie down in green pastures, He leads me beside quiet waters, He restores my soul."

Clouds rolled through to steal the final layer of our sunshine fleece. "He guides me along the right paths for His name's sake."

Full-body spasms set in. "And I…will dwell…in the house of the Lord… for…ev…er."[1]

After a short pause and a long stare, shivering and shaking, Ada asked, "Dad, can we go dwell in a warm house now?"

Serendipity[2] is a funny thing. I had intended to connect the dots between Shepherd God, the ultimate guide, and Ada's journey through the wilds of first grade. Instead, while finishing our Frostys and psalm in the blazing heat of the car, her thoughts shifted toward others—families that won't get to crank the heat on high when the winds whip up and the kids in her school without snow gloves, winter hats, and Costanza-like GORE-TEX for when the weather gets dicey.

I was leading us to the plush green pasture in those Christian paintings with lambs and laughing kids and halos, but Ada, without intending to, steered us toward something more valuable in the moment. A better image. A greater path into righteousness.

Serendipity.

I have a basic rule of thumb in our one-on-ones: don't force it. I bring something to the table, a verse or a topic or a story, and I show up prepared because I value my kids and the Word. It's a special time, unique and filled to the brim with legacy. But I'm also learning to trust the Spirit when He sparks an idea beyond my files. I like watching their minds work too. Especially Ada's. Ada looks lost at first, stares right through me. Her lips purse, her eyebrows fold in and then her eyes begin to jet back and forth, searching. That's her way of connecting the dots within. One dot in Psalm 23 with a string stretching out to another dot in the cold Ohio winds, wrapped around tight and then outstretched to the final dot of families without homes and heat.

We're learning to **serve**[3]. In small capacities more often than not, like picking up trash in the neighborhood and performing general handyman work for a few seniors. It's not as sexy as rescuing people from starvation, sure, but there's something about serving others, no matter how invisible the act, that fills our purpose tanks beyond our understanding. It's as if the Spirit of the Living God emanates from our work offerings and then, maybe through osmosis, seeps into our hearts. Tangible righteousness, I suppose.

"Dad, I think I have an extra pair of snow gloves. Can we give them to someone who needs them tomorrow?" Psalm 23 serendipitously at work. The Shepherd had fixed us up with gloves like green fields. More gloves than we needed. The question was, would we act like under-shepherds and share them with a kid in need?

It's an awesome sight to behold a young soul grasping, maybe for the first time, the practical kindness of sacrificial giving, isn't it? One year earlier and she wasn't yet personally invested. Willing? Sure, but not practically engaged. But, in this moment, shivering in the final throes of winter with a gritty image of God at work in our mess, she could see the dots forming and falling into place.

She physically felt the need.

Remember when Jesus spit in the mud and wiped it on the dude's eyes?[4] Or when He put His hands on the crippled woman, freeing her to stand up straight for the first time in eighteen years?[5] When our mindset changes and our heart leaves the Joneses behind, what do our hands do? Some of us keep on coddling the phone, polishing the samovar and caressing our own bodies in that van down by the river. But for others, you and me, our hands show up to the table with divine healing, food from the garden, calluses from service and gloves for the little girl who's never had a pair to call her own.

I hadn't orchestrated that serendipitous discovery, but I loved jumping in on the journey. To be honest, I've already forced too many conversations, and it's becoming increasingly unsettling to catch that reflection in the rearview mirror of a dad who has shifted mid-conversation from curious to killjoy. I bet I'm alone in this, right? You can imagine, though, that those were not the most enjoyable connects for anyone involved.

Yeah, I may have missed a few dozen ahas in the past, but I'll take these winter revivals no matter how frosty they are. After all, Ada's only just begun the journey.

/ / /

My kids are young, for now. I find it important to stress this when sharing discoveries about the spiritual and relational rhythms of fatherhood. I simply don't have decades of wisdom to lean on, and there's a difference, I know. There's a natural trust due the sage-like wisdom of grandparents several generations on with all the bumps, bruises and blessings that healthy and even hurting kids provide.

But there's also something revealing about partnering with someone early on in the journey. Someone who is wrestling with the same scenarios or who is a small step or two ahead. Some of the sweetest connections I've had as a dad, even temporary ones set apart for a season or a struggle, have been those formed with other young dads. There's no shortage of wounds and questions and encouragement. We ask and offer. We vent and listen.

"So, you know we're working through a discipline game plan, right? Tell me, how do you process the whole tender defender role? You know, gentle discipline, silly and serious? I'm beginning to think Brooke and I might not actually be studying the same page."

"Can I say this without sounding like a braggadocios butt-crack dad? My kids are freakin' awesome on the court! Super coolheaded. Great teamsmanship. And they practice hard."

"Hey, just calling to let you know that I'm taking a long walk, grabbing some fresh air and asking the Lord to calm me down before I go home and swat some hindquarters."

And it's not because any one of us is particularly wise, it's just that it's tangible. Breathing the same struggles and salvaging the same joys, even for a melancholic recovering killjoy, is like a nightly shot of that divine top shelf. The Spirit makes His presence known, if only for a moment. It's a soul-lifting moment.

Salvage[6] is an important word to lean on here. The word saved gets thrown around a lot in the Christian sphere, and it should. It's direct and true, and it's precisely what Christ offers us, salvation. But salvage is good too. It feels grittier in some ways, doesn't it?

My doomsday issues, my funks, my killjoy attitudes—it's these that I'm salvaged from. Life in a junkyard of crap thinking, self-deprecation and incessant internal lies. Christ salvages me, like the wreckage of a ruined car now redeemed and repurposed for a new and endless adventure. Maybe it just feels manlier to say I've been salvaged.

I get to do this as a life coach. We spend time salvaging healthy dreams from the wreckage of failure and confusion and indecision.

As coach dad? Yeah, salvaging operations run day and night.

I salvage crumpled-up math problems.

I salvage fun tossed out in the, "I just don't get it."

I salvage confidence when the longboard flies down the road and my son's on his back.

I salvage hope when it gets lost in the gut-churning, "Why did they make fun of me, dad?"

I salvage trust when I'm louder and angrier than could ever be necessary and then sincerely and deeply apologize on the side of their bed with tears.

I salvage habits and hobbies and projects and discussions gone awry.

And as a husband? Well, Brooke is quite adept at managing the spiritual undertones of reduce, reuse and recycle when it comes to my steps and strides. She is a sacrificial salvager.

Truth is, we salvage because we've been divinely and undeservingly salvaged. That's what the **Savior**[7] does, and when the Creator Savior models something, it's worth adopting. He rescues from the wreck. He redeems from the ruin. He, well…go ahead and alliterate any number of salvific phrases here. My point is, those of us who cry out to Him from the junkyard, we know what it feels like to be salvaged, so we join in.

/ / /

"You prepare a table before me…You anoint my head with oil; my cup overflows."[8]

The car was toasty, the windows fogging over and my cup was overflowing. The Lord set the table, and Ada serendipitously salvaged what I brought to share. Awesome. No, my head wasn't anointed with oil, but a Frosty, my daughter and a psalm? Totally righteous connect if you ask me.

T

Thankfully Terrified

Trials are the secret sauce.

I'm sure most of you reading this will push back, maybe even throw this lexicon at the wall and demand I admit that love, not struggle, is the secret sauce. You can say that. I might even agree on a good day. But this tension, this struggle to define the ingredients of life's secret sauce, may actually support my point.

Besides, love is too obvious.

"Love the Lord your God with your whole being."[1]

"Love your neighbor—yep, even *that* neighbor—with the same love you show yourself."[2]

"And now I will show you the most excellent way."[3]

"God is love."[4]

Okay, that last one isn't fair. It's obvious John was getting a little carried away by the Spirit by that point in his letter. Nonetheless, I'll admit that love, divine love, love sourced in Creator-Savior God, a love more potent than KFC's eleven secret herbs and spices, is more poignant than struggle. But here's the catch: love isn't a secret, is it?

We all know this "secret." It's in everything from Grammy's banana bread to our willingness to step in front of a bullet for our kids. We know that infants need to feel, hear and drink love. That kids need loving discipline when they sass up a room. That loving guidance is vital for the heart and mind through dating and degrees, but also in the kitchen when our kids want Rocky Road sprinkled with Nerds for breakfast. Maybe Rocky Road with caramel drizzle, but Nerds?

Love is anything but a secret. We may fail to offer it, show it, model it, or accept it, but there it is, ready for the taking.

No, the real secret sauce is the collection of **trials**[5] we navigate on our way toward our bandera of dreams.

The thing about an authentic secret sauce isn't so much that it exists but how it's applied, tasted and treated. Those eleven herbs and spices are handled with care. They're planned and processed, and they put their flavor where my mouth is.

Throughout the story of God, humanity experiences both internal and external trials, ravaging and revealing. If you're like me, there are times when you drop to your knees in frustration. Other times, you drop in submission, plead for support, or simply offer quiet, weathered whispers of praise.

Isn't it strange how the inconvenience of spilling coffee on a good day swells into a crisis on a rough one? Or how a struggle with alcohol might sink your boat, yet never be more than a gentle wake beneath mine?

Of course there are those awful positions we find ourselves trapped in for a season without an obvious exit. Trials beyond our grasp. Like that final notice in the mail before eviction. Or the pink slip before Christmas. Or a positive test result for that routine exam.

But it's not really just a trial, is it?

James, the late-to-the-game half-brother of Jesus, shed some light on what's really going on: "Consider it pure joy, my brothers and sisters, whenever you face trials of many kinds, because you know that the testing of your faith develops perseverance. Oh yeah, and perseverance must finish its work so that you may become mature and complete."[6] Do you see it? A trial isn't just a trial, it's a **test**[7].

I spent years pushing back on that view. I think in my stubborn pity I wanted to believe that some trials are nothing more than a broken world chewing us up and spitting us out. Undivine and impersonal. But James pushes back on me by using a word that weaves together trial with temptation and testing. Which means that a trial isn't just a difficult event, but one that personally tempts my sensibilities while testing my faithful ability to stay on mission, morally weigh the options, and reach for the Creator. All while suffering.

And it's not just the big tests, either. It's my response to another spilled coffee. Or my attitude in the face of the total demolition of a dream.

Struggle that ends in a doomsday of the heart isn't much of a sauce worth bringing to the party, is it? On the other hand, a secret sauce discovered in the persistent throes of a trial, one that tests every ounce of our being? That's a recipe worth sharing. Why? Because you and I "know that suffering produces perseverance, and perseverance, character; and character, hope."[8]

And hope tastes good.

It's why handsome protagonists in movies eat and snack and sip in every scene. No, it's not just to fill space or offer movement in monologue or give their hands something to do. It's because hope is nourishment. Hope sustains life. Food embodies hope.

The secret sauce has taken on a whole new tangy flavor, hasn't it?

Can you imagine what our daily frustrations would taste like through this recipe? How freeing it would be to actually count it all joy? To believe that trials, those we've conjured up in our selfish scheming, as well as those heaped on us, can be worked into the meat of life like a secret sauce and grilled to perfection? Awesome.

/ / /

When was the last time you were **terrified**⁹? I don't mean like that time you saw The Blair Witch Project in theaters thinking it was a documentary only to curl up in the fetal position beneath the seat, covered in popcorn and rolling around in spilled Pepsi. No, not that sort of terror. I mean the kind of dread ushered in by a trial before you remember that hope and joy and perseverance and victory are part of the journey. That moment you realize you've cheated or when eviction looms large or when you realize that God's forgiveness really is that extraordinary and you have to go have a conversation with someone. That kind of terror.

Terror is emotional, isn't it? To be terrified is to be overwhelmed with fear. That overwhelming state of mind is physically exhausting. Sometimes that fear propels us to run away. Sometimes it paralyzes. Sometimes it launches us toward the source of the fear like Joanna running into my arms when I growl like a bear. No matter how we respond to a terrifying trial, it has spiritual implications.

When I lost my position in ministry, strained close relationships and internally tanked six months after purchasing my first home, and all this eleven months after moving my family to a new state, yeah, I was terrified. Horrified. Mortified. All of those -ified words that fit this sort of worst-case scenario nightmare for a melancholist. Which only fosters that ongoing "If I'd only..." debilitating internal dialogue that wells up when we haven't prepared for the test.

It was a month before I accepted those trials as something greater and several years before I began to breathe again. But it wasn't until around the third month that terror rolled in like a freight train. I could feel the rumble drawing near. I could taste the rust and salt as it barreled through. My spirit took the brunt of the full-frontal crash, thank God. But my old bandera shredded like confetti in the fallout. In survival mode, my body was forced to act even before my mind was willing. That's the way of terror; it forces movement. We're actually wired this way.

I had a choice to make. We all do in these instances. I could let terror spur me outward and away from my current reality. Try to run from funk, faith and family. Or press into it. Push through the fear into the heart of the wreckage, tear open the dining car and take a huge bite out of those baking ribs covered in secret sauce.

Sounds like an action movie, doesn't it? Sounds adventurous and heroic. In real life, it sucks. It sucks all the air out of the room. It sucked the energy out of every limb in my body just to make it one step closer to the source. It sucked the feeling of hope out of prayer. Confrontation takes work. Yeah with another human, but also with our past, with our current hurts and with the God who, as I grasped not so long ago, truly is with us in the middle of it all.

It sucks, but facing a trial head on, terrified, really is the work of a hero. Ask one and they'll say, "I was just doing the right thing when the moment called for it." And then they'll look you in the eye, take a deep breath and add, "You would do the same thing." And they believe it.

Do you?

Do you actually believe that you and I can be everyday heroes? Heroes to our kids. Noble spouses. Character-driven leaders accepting the test in front of us, snagging a handful of cashews from the bowl on the bar top and diving in with fireproof pants full of hope.

We can.

Even when the right decision takes years to bring a trial into the light of victory?

We can.

And when the quagmire seems too grimy to bear?

We grin and bear the muck while reaching for the Spirit like a struggling sloth fallen from his perch. We can do this because we know what trials are really all about.

The overall trajectory? Forward. One terrifying test at a time.

What's interesting is just how uplifting this process is. Remember Paul's description of the raw impact of his own trials? "But even if I am being poured out like a drink offering on the sacrifice and service coming from your faith, I'm glad and rejoice with all of you."[10] Poured out like a drink offering? Glad? Rejoicing?

I get it now.

Paul was so focused on The Bandera of Banderas that to him, living as a sacrifice, and even dying as a martyr, was simply part of the fabric of that journey. And he was **thankful**[11] for every thread.

Poured out like a drink.

Washed away like a spilled glass of wine over a stone altar.

Thankful for the opportunity to suffer.

Thankful for all of the divine testing because of the depth of faith and character and joy being produced.

Paul wasn't a masochist.[12] He wasn't chasing after trials for self-gratification. No, he was whipped, beaten, shipwrecked, bitten by a poisonous snake, mobbed, stoned and he spent the better part of his later years under house arrest and in prison for the sake of divine fulfillment. Most believe he was eventually martyred for his faith too. Paul wasn't grasping for some perverted form of pleasure. He was thankful for the opportunity to suffer like Jesus. Thankful for the ability to persevere under immense pressure to quit, submit and recant. He was thankful for the encouragement his faith-filled trials brought others. And he was thankful for the ability to share the secret sauce of trials with brothers and sisters struggling under the weight of their own testing.

No doubt many of you can relate to Paul. You've lived your own terrifying trials worth their weight in Sweet Baby Ray's. There's hope in that sauce, isn't there?

Several years ago, Brooke and I separately came to the conclusion that thankfulness needed to be our family theme for a year. Over the next year, we rediscovered the power of thankfulness as an uncanny antidote to funk, a gentle motivator when terror bares its teeth. Through Paul's experiences we could sense that thankfulness would foster a fresh season in pursuit of everything good and true and pure and right and awesome, no matter the paralyzing depth of inevitable quagmires ahead.

Turns out, thankfulness is another savory herb in the secret sauce of trial.

/ / /

Maybe it's worth pausing for a minute right here, right now, and praying for wisdom in the trial shaking the ground beneath our feet. Praying that thankfulness would prop us up under the logs bowing our shoulders.

A little hope in the trial. A spoonful of perseverance in the test. A cup of thankfulness in the struggle, sprinkled and slathered over those ribs waiting to be baked and shared. Maybe it's time you create your own secret sauce.

U

Uniquely un-Useless

Years ago I started digging into Christology, a thick word for the study of the Christ. Just below the surface, I struck this wild term, *hypostatic union*, and it kicked me around. It sounded both overly technical and theologically heavy. I felt small. How could my small-town life—my world of pulling weeds under a hot sun, changing diapers in the middle of family movie night and wading through the quagmire of self-deprecation—coexist with this level of theology? Turns out, a little curiosity goes a long way.

Hypo is a prefix meaning "beneath" or "within." Think of the last time your nurse practitioner took a blood sample. Can you feel the hypodermic needle sliding under your skin? Me too. You probably can't tell, but I just blacked out for a minute.

Hyper is the exact opposite of *hypo*, and it means "over" and "excessive." I absolutely despise the prefix *hyper*. It's overused, overvalued, beyond descriptive, excessively hyped and generally unnecessary everywhere it attaches itself to a word. Like *hyperbole*. *Hypo*, on the other hand, offers a flavor of humility in its beneathness. My kind of word.

Static, the second part of the equation, is all about remaining in place. Fixed and steadfast.

And then there's *union*. **Union**[1] conveys the idea of two things becoming one. United.

Hypostatic union is one of those Koine Greek terms pressed into high-level theology, translated into tenured collegiate English, dissected, debated and eventually experienced. Essentially, it's an intense way of describing the divinity of God contained within the flesh of Jesus here on earth. Not like dressing within a turkey, and more than basting the outside with delicious juices, but a genuinely mysterious merging of two totally different natures pressed uniformly into one divine being.

It's startling to look back on the past and see that Jesus said as much, minus the turkey: "But in these last days He has spoken to us through His Son, the One He appointed heir of all things, and through whom He made the universe. The Son is the radiance of God's glory and the exact representation of his being [nature and personhood], sustaining all things by his powerful word."[2] Catch that? The hypostatic union explained to a haphazard band of Jewish believers and slowly carving its way into the minds of a bunch of beer-drinking, pig-farming, English-speaking disciples centuries later. Jesus, the exact radiant image of God's divine nature, here in the dirt wearing a flesh suit.

Spirit and flesh. Faith and deed. Supernatural and natural. The God-man.

I think union is becoming a lost art. Sure, that deep union between humanity and Creator God, but I guess I'm thinking more specifically about the gritty, divinity-wrapped union in marriage. I know, I know, it's a topic that stirs some to burn their dresses and slacks like bras and flags. Others, I suppose, are prone to tote around heavy bags full of pain, confusion and turmoil. And still others blush and sigh with a sense of security or redemption. No matter the course, *gritty* is still the word I choose to describe the beautiful mess of marriage.

I was thinking about the awesome power within this union, how Brooke and I are united on this lifelong journey through ditches and diamonds (more ditches than diamonds). We're two **unique**[3] individuals breathing the breath of God as one unit. A couple without equal among couples simply because our union exists between one uniquely somber Rich and one uniquely gracious Brooke. No one else will live our lives, entangle themselves together in the same ditches we have or witness the uniqueness of our kids in private.

"Hey, Dad, remember this?" Elias asked in passing. "Ya'll wanna come back 'round here and git yerself some chicken 'n be-yis-cuts!"

I raised an eyebrow.

He stared. "Chicken 'n beee-yiiisssss-cuts!"

Private family jokes outstaying their welcome, yet endlessly unifying.

More than ever I'm intrigued by the multiplying effect of this union. Brooke and I became one fleshly unit joined together with Christ in a spiritual bond of three, and in the blink of an eye three kids emerged and now we're six. I know I'm pressing in on a Seuss-like territory here, but this is where the marriage analogy gets gritty, isn't it? One day we woke up in a ditch with a biscuit in one hand and a diamond in the other.

The truth is, that "one day" was really fourteen years in the making. It was a long series of one days.

I promised to journey alongside Brooke by word and deed. *Union.*

I promised to lead and love my kids through birth. *Hypo.*

I promised my life and rhythm to my God in belief and profession. *Static.*

I think this is the lost art I'm grasping for. A heaven-and-earth unity. It's incredible how many times a broken heart, dream, vocation or relationship has fogged up the mountaintop view of deep and divine unity in my life. And rather than wipe off the window for clarity, I've closed the curtains, sat in the dark and nursed the funk.

This kind of unity and the brokenness that emerges and entangles isn't limited to the marriage bed, is it? No doubt we all have experiences with gritty unions that go up in flames like drought-ridden forests. We've experienced fatherlessness, abuse, sexual perversion, financial wreckage, hopelessness, unhealthy expectations, prejudice, broken self-image, the list goes on.

Thank God His unity with us never ends.

Thank God tomorrow is another opportunity for an aha.

Thank God for the unique, undiscovered unions, the bridges yet to be built and rebuilt, the high-flying banderas waiting to be raised high.

If the union of heaven and earth in the life of Jesus is any sort of symbol for the beauty and uniqueness of a healthy bond, then I want the thickest, tightest unions with the people closest to me.

/ / /

It's absurd how quickly I'll buy into feeling **useless**[4]. Embarrassing, really. Little more than a tone of disapproval or the rejection of an idea and I sink into a quagmire of killed joy. Even as a kid I would sneak off to a hidden space to regroup. I'd find an unlocked car in the driveway, spin the chrome handle and plastic maroon knob with both hands to roll the window down and wait in silence.

Wait for the feeling to pass.

Wait for a purpose or a goal or a hope to emerge.

Wait for Mom to check the pulse of my soul.

It's absurd how many useless ruts my brain has formed over the years. In fact, they're ditches at this point, eroded by the seemingly endless torrential downpour of negative self-talk. I think this is why the hypostatic union blew my mind. Not only is the Creator Christ a perfect blend of heaven and earth, but I am the living and breathing overflow of that divine blend through faith.

More than a rewiring of the heart and soul, those ditches have become a full-on construction site, rerouting funk, bottlenecking deception and adding new, unhindered channels for clarity and truth and light. I think this is what Paul was describing in his letter to Philemon. One of Philemon's slaves had become a disciple of Paul's, a new blend of heaven and earth, during a stint in prison, and Paul deeply appreciated his partnership. Writing to Philemon, Paul said, "At one point Onesimus your slave was useless to you, a disobedient rebel, but now he has become useful to both you and me."[5]

Onesimus, whose name actually translates as "useful," had become useless to Philemon. Not only is it the perfect play-on-name dad joke for a teenage daughter's prom date, but it's a great analogy for us in recapturing the depth of our divine value baked into our very names. Names mean things, sure, but to Jesus every name holds unique value.

Onesimus was useful. Period.

For crying out loud, his parents named him Useful. As a dad I can feel the hopes and prayers for his life bubbling up before birth. I have no idea if Onesimus had been a slave from the womb or if some personal disaster brought him into that miserable walk, but as a runaway slave, in Philemon's eyes, he had become an entirely useless source of manpower, a financial loss. Thank God his story didn't end there, right? How amazing is it that while on the run he's united with Paul, partnered on the unique mission of sharing the freedom Creator Christ offers? To Paul, this slave with a new sense of being became a vessel filled to the brim with benefit. The exact opposite of what Philemon saw.

Can you picture a Paul in your life? How about a Philemon? It's a terrifying thought that through bitterness or pain or even stubbornness I could become a Philemon to my own kids. I could fail to see them as useful, vital, and divinely valuable right here and right now. But it's equally inspiring to own the potential of seeing the kids under my roof through the lens of Paul, which is really the point of view of Christ.

But Paul doesn't merely accept Onesimus as a useful partner. No, he fights for this guy's freedom like a brother. Paul pleads and barters and guilt-trips Philemon into accepting Onesimus as a usefully redeemed brother of his own: "I hope you will choose to be as useful to me here in prison, just as your very useful slave has become. Listen, you would breathe life into my soul accepting Onesimus as a brother."[6] Bold, isn't it? Not gutsy in an out-of-line sort of way, just a deep understanding of God's union with humanity and a willingness to put his relationship on the line for another.

I love this piece of history. I'm thankful that this ancient interaction between godly men working through such a gritty subject is alive and available. I've never been a slave to another—my stomach turns at the thought—but I've been enslaved to lies, lusts, hurts and struggles. The ditches in my brain show the old scars.

Like Onesimus in his fresh start, I no longer wait for the false sense of uselessness to pass. I don't expect another to check on the state of my soul. Brooke does, of course. Her deep care is the divine overflow of her unique union with me. But I don't wait for it. I wake up, swing my feet to the floor, raise the bandera of dreams high above the fray and take my unique position to do what only I can do. It may take a day or two in a funk before I'm able to see the bandera clearly, but that beats a lifetime of groping about in a useless fog.

/ / /

How are you investing in your most intimate unions?

Can you see them?

These unions matter. They matter because you and I aren't useless. They matter because Christ's hypostatic union demonstrates their divine value. The more we shift our language, inside and out, the more new grooves our mindset carves into our brain and the more successful we'll be at ushering in the advent of hope and thankfulness. It's a freeing thought, isn't it? So, what about those unions?

V

Villainized Values

Years ago, a stocky little Elias and I were hanging out at the royal Burger King. Cold drinks on call, Bibles open, nuggets and fries on the tray with a ketchup runway smeared across the paper mat. (I get carried away with ketchup.) Vines and branches were the topic of the day. I'd been looking forward to sketching fun images, connecting spiritual dots, and maybe pruning some limbs, ya know? Manly things over mass-produced, deep-fried nuggets.

Sipping my Dr. Pepper, I was drumming on about these vines and branches, how "God trims off every branch in us that doesn't bear fruit." [1]Hearing a curious shuffle, I looked up. "Right, buddy?"

Elias, caught in the middle of an uncontrollable wiggle, glanced my way.

"He prunes so that we'll grow stronger and healthier. Catch that, dude?" Nope. Dude wasn't in on any of it. The little man was having a dance fight with himself in the enormous tinted window at the end of our table overlooking a packed Chipotle patio.

Funtastic! I thought. *Kids squirm. It's how they focus, right?* "So, bud, why do you think the vine is so important to the branches?"

This kid must be super focused busting all those moves.

"Branches? Vine? Deep Christological insights from garden to Gardener?" Squinting, my curiosity gave way to its nemesis: control.

So I've mentioned my one-on-one rule of thumb, right? That forcing deep spiritual conversations is about as fruitful as forcing a bell pepper to ripen. Yeah, that gold nugget of wisdom was birthed over these fried nuggets of disappointment.

"Sit. Down."

Squished in total surprise, Elias's spirit melted. Another grease stain on the bench.

"We're having a deep discussion about Christlike character," I gurgled through a sip of my medium-size Dr. P, the contempt thick in my voice.

His wiggling feet twitched, sort of how I imagine a body might in cardiac arrest. Those wild giggles choked off with a whimper.

I leaned back to watch the smoke clear. Dance fight over.

Elias: KO'd.

Dad: Disqualified.

You can imagine how joyful our faith-filled discoveries were for the rest of the evening. Yeah, me neither. It's deeply unsettling being guilty of chopping the head off one of my own core **values**[2]—you know, those handful of principles that model and shape and guide our life rhythm. I hold in high esteem these divine connects with my kids. So when the gurgling of momentary disdain melts their little frame, I'm not sure who crawls away worse for the wear.

How great would it be to pull out a souped-up DeLorean, toss in a few dirty socks, punch in that time and date, and head back for a do-over? If I could, I'd go back and challenge that little guy to a dance battle right there on those greasy plastic benches. "Hey, dude, have you heard this through the grapevine?" I would say with that perfect dad-joke straight face. Then I'd follow it with three minutes of mirrored shimmy-shaking, a small offering that would have granted another fifteen of eye-to-eye insights filled to the top of his poofy hair with hope.

I'm told DeLoreans are impossible to find. Time machines aren't so prevalent either.

Developing a fresh lexicon has the added benefit of expanding my view of the intricate connections between words and actions. Not only am I digesting fresh words that nourish my soul, but I'm also beginning to grasp the tangible depth these words have to offer those around me. Unfortunately time travel isn't commercially viable yet, but this doesn't mean I can't reclaim a dance fight.

The Creator of time and space isn't oblivious to our endless desire for a DeLorean. There's this whole other set of tools He's developed as an alternative to time travel. As exciting? No, not in the moment. But as beneficial as a redo? Yeah, I think so. In fact, the potential for greater relational depth and divine insight is exponential. Struggle in redemption is unifying.

Forgiveness is an incredibly powerful tool. I can't unsquish Elias, but I can own my muck, repent, apologize and ask that little dude to forgive me. I'll never forget the first time I did this. Sitting on the side of his bed, voice shaking, I was terrified. Yet he was so eager to forgive.

And then there's the tool of tomorrow. Of course, tomorrow isn't promised. I realize that. But planning for it while there's still a today seems wise, doesn't it? I can do the gritty work of rehabbing my expectations before we meet again. I can invite my dude to explore divine creation with me again. I can attempt to reinflate him with the hope of Christ through the gentle word of a dad who loves him and his inherent quirkiness. I can.

No, tomorrow isn't a guarantee, but if it shows up I want to be caught without shoes on. Found in the garden straddling my values with one bare foot on grace and the other in the soil of what could be. After all, no one stops watering their garden simply because tomorrow might not happen.

Let's be honest about time travel, anyhow: I'd screw up something else only to regret it and circle back for another attempt. We've all seen "documentaries" about these endless loops of unintended consequences: *Terminator, Back to the Future, Looper*, and, of course, *Bill and Ted's Excellent Adventure*.

I imagine this is how we end up squishing and squashing those we love. We're so busy struggling to control time and space with our invisible DeLoreans that we forget to take a deep breath, say, "I'm wildly sorry. Will you forgive me?" and look ahead with purpose.

James brought this little quagmire to light when he said, "What causes fights and feuds among you? It's that your passions are at war within you, right? You desire something and don't get what you want."[3]

I squished my kindergartner because of a half-baked idea I had about how one-on-one connects should work and flow and look from the outside. I jumped into pruning before any of the growth. Actually, that wasn't even pruning. Pruning is about the health of the plant, not the overreaction of an angry gardener. Meanwhile, that little boy had an unwavering idea of what quality time with his dad could look like and he didn't get to experience it either. Turns out, Elias was living our family values in an infinitely purer way than I could have imagined. And I didn't even notice.

It sucks realizing you're the **villain**[4]. Another double-edged lampoon in the back at the hands of Scoundrel Killjoy, the ultimate dream-crushing naysayer. It's a painful thing to discover and come to terms with, though in my case—yours too, I imagine—it didn't take much convincing. The pile of toddler mush in front of me was quite villainously descriptive.

I like the word *villain*. It doesn't get used in real life, ya know? It's a movie character. Animated and exaggerated and stereotyped. And when I layer that cartoony image of Scoundrel Killjoy with the fruit of the sinful nature Paul wrote about—hatred, jealousy and fits of rage[5]— my stomach turns.

So, I made a rule of thumb to help guide our dance-talks over fries and coffee:

1. Have fun. Enjoy the ride.

2. Don't force it. Let the Holy Spirit guide our time together.

I didn't want to be the villain. I really, really didn't want to be the villain in my own home. Still don't. I want the legacy of a hero, if only under my roof. I want to be the dad in a spandex jumper and cape, partnered side by side with his amazing wife in leading their family to that victorious bandera. I want those deeper conversations with Elias while he's young. While he's mine.

/ / /

From my perch, there are days when it's nearly impossible to get this right, to see across the table with all these logs in my eyes. I wonder if villainy is nothing more than the overflow of logs jamming up our view of truth, bottlenecking a fuller understanding of Christlikeness. How freeing it would be to toss them on the fire, enjoy a rum and Coke and roast s'mores with the kids.

Turns out, I'm the one being pruned on the vine. My kids have a way of setting up serendipitous encounters. Maybe I'm not a full-fledged villain after all, only acting the part as dead limbs are revealed, broken off, and tossed in with the logs. Dead wood sounds more useful this way, doesn't it? I'm beginning to see how the light shining within combines with the glow of those burning limbs to reveal the values worth living and breathing. I suppose the rule of thumb is simply another way of saying, "Hey, Rich, trust the Gardener. In this world you'll have trouble—logs and limbs and raging fires—but take heart, He's overcome those very raging fires."[6]

No doubt if I take heart now I'll look back on these troubles twenty years down the road and laugh one of those robust Santa Claus laughs at the memory of this kindergartener's busting moves while sketching spiritual truths. That's victory. I *can* experience that.

So, what's your rule of thumb these days?

W

Wild Wisdom

This ancient word of **wisdom**[1] has been creeping into my mind lately. No doubt you've heard it—Proverbs 22:6—it's probably stale as bread around your dinner table: "Train up your daughter in the way she should go, and when she's old she won't depart from it."[2]

I'm beginning to sense that my entire lexiconical adventure these past several years revolves around this ancient familial discipleship rhythm. These words and the actions birthed from their refreshed insights are ingredients in the simmering cauldron of this season's soup, raising my kids.

That stale-as-bread insight seems to be finding new life in this aging pot.

Reminds me of the first week I ever spent in the Outer Banks. Brooke and I had been dating for nearly a year when her parents invited me, cautiously, to join in on the fun for a few days. I ended up flying down with a couple of friends who were also invited.

It was the first time I'd seen a kitchen on the third story. Not one of those tiny, New York apartment–style kitchens, but a full-blown, open-air, spring-break kitchen. A kitchen for healthy people, I guess. People like me prefer a kitchen on the first floor. Snacks after swimming should not require a gauntlet of steps to the heavens. Otherwise, it was a laid-back, comfortable, half-week stretch of an Ernest-goes-camping-with-the-Fockers scenario. Only with more grace and no hidden cameras.

Every night, dinner was prepped, served and enjoyed together family style. And each meal was delicious, but the final one has stuck with me. With plans to head out early Saturday morning and Friday reserved for an epic seafood night, Thursday's dinner was left to wilds of the remaining grocery scraps: cheese, onions, some dried up bread etc.

"You know what you do with stale French bread, right?" Bob asked.

"Ducks?"

"Soup," he said, bringing water to a boil while warming the oven. Bob is a family friend, one of those guys who radiates the wisdom of God.

I don't remember playing any role in the preparation of that meal. Odds are I headed off to get schooled in shuffleboard by some anonymous retired couple. I can still smell the incredible aroma filling that beach house from the top floor down, though.

Sweet onions like noodles.

Beef stock.

Gooey cheeses crisped to perfection.

Thick and flavorful bread.

I'd never had anything like it. I was a clam chowder in a can kinda guy. Onions? Repurposed stale bread? I know, I know, some of you super delicate chefs are hung up on my canned clam chowder past and panicking over the use of stale bread for such a divinely orchestrated meal. I might consider backing off the canned chowder, but I won't back down from the bread. Bob and his old family recipe made me a believer.

I think this is what that ancient proverb has begun stirring deep down in my gut. It's an unsettling reminder that my words, living and breathing words, are in the process of building up my kids for the journey of a lifetime. Like speaking a sort of French onion soup. Reclaimed and repurposed stale truths reinvigorated and winning others over in real time.

Soup makes wisdom sound civil, don't you think? It feels tame. But I'm not so sure that it is.

There's something mildly barbaric about making use of old, stale food for the main course in what rounds out to be a five-star feast. Personally, I'm drawn to that sort of edible pragmatism. A delectable subversion of high-brow expectations in the face of limited resources.

We see this sort of wild wisdom in the rhythm and rhyme of Christ: "Go sell all you have. Eat my flesh. Drink my blood. You wanna follow me? Know this, birds have homes, not me. Carry your own cross. Leave your coat and wallet and let's go. Don't worry, I'm going with you."[3] Listen, I'm not trying to tug on any particular blue- and white-collar guilt strings here. After all, I'm sipping coffee at a seventies-era table I got for free and spent a year refinishing in my unelectrified garage. I'm simply saying that wisdom found in stale truths is often reignited in the gutter with a divine spark. It springs to life in the scraps and leftovers. It rises from the muck, shakes off the rotten bits and simmers into a soup worth slurping.

I think that's parenting too.

We're tired and hurt and foggy-minded, I know, but how much longer are we going to be the most influential adults shaping boundaries in the lives under our roofs? Talk about an aha! You and I, we have intimate access to true wisdom on the vine. Let's drop the canned chowder already, raise the new recipe high and whip up some tasty meals.

"Live that way and I'll tell you what," Jesus says, "I'll see you in paradise."[4]

/ / /

"How was school, dude? Anything wild happen?"

I like the latter question there. I ask it all the time.

"How was the bike ride, little lady? Anything wild on the path?"

I ask it so often that to my kids it becomes stale as bread. But then something wild does happen, and for a season the question is full of life again.

Wild[5] is a word wrapped up with different meanings depending on one's perspective. For instance, ask a kid raised deep in the gut of the inner city by a single, hard-working mom, full of hope yet thrown around on a tumultuous journey from one apartment to the next, and "Anything wild happen today?" will conjure up some very specific memories and feelings.

On the other side of town, ask the same question to a kid afforded the opportunity to grab another adventure with her alcoholic dad to another city in another country by another private jet to another luxury hotel for a business meeting and some "family time" and you know what? "Anything wild happen today?" will stir up an entirely different set of emotions and images.

Most days I'm met with a "nothing really" or a "just the usual." But every once in a while something beyond the normal kicks up some passion, some curiosity for that deeper slice of life, and I get to hear, "Actually..."

"Actually" is a great response, isn't it? As a parent I love this break in the routine. Yeah, it might be followed by a "I've been suspended for cheating on my self-portrait in art class," but more often than not it's something worth teasing out, pressing into and celebrating.

"Actually, I crashed my scooter on the way to school, tore up my shin, bloodied my lip and still made it to class on time."

"Dude, way to persevere!" Seriously. How cool is that? I would have crawled into a ditch for a few hours out of sheer embarrassment at that age. Tucked within his wild actually is a passion for life and learning untethered from the choking chains of peer pressure and intersectional victimhood and easy excuses.

"Actually, I talked with my friends about heaven today."

"Really? That's awesome! How did that come about?"

"Well, we were walking around the playground trying to find something to do, and since I've been thinking about what the kingdom of heaven is like, well, I just asked my friends what they thought."

Elias rocks back and forth a little when his wild mind is firing on all cylinders, as though his body begins the conversation before handing over control to his mouth.

And when Ada is processing a thought, her hands lock together, lips purse and her brows furrow ever so slightly. With her eyes uncomfortably shifting, nervous yet excited to bare her mind, she gently and passionately invites you into her curious thinking machine.

This kind of wild doesn't foster chaos. These wild moments, tucked within the realm of our daily rhythm, are full of depth and insight. Truly wild moments offer something to the one living the wild ride but also to those within earshot. There's often a witness to the wild, isn't there?

I've witnessed my kids body surf in the Atlantic, zip line through trees, boldly take on adulting challenges, navigate capital cities on foot and dive into new faith communities without hesitation. And you know what? This sort of wild fosters wisdom. This sort of wild looks around and pulls together a French onion soup worth flaunting before the Soup Nazi. Delicious meals aren't produced through chaotic confusion in the kitchen, they're pulled together by wildly noble legends willing to live out the answer to a stale question, "Anything wild happen?"

Parenting, the kind of wild parenting you and I want to live, requires this sort of intentionality. I think most of us want the adventure bubbling beneath the conventional surface of our daily rhythm. We're eager to hear our kids tell us a story—a good story, an uplifting story that pushes us to greater heights. And yes, I'm including you in this too. I know, you're a soul-to-skin melancholic by blood and design, but even you are hungry for a better world of words on adventure.

I know I am.

And most of the time it starts with purpose. We're propelled toward our bandera, which continues to inspire these wild dreams of something more. These dreams spill over onto our kids in the form of curious questions and hope-filled attitudes. After all, chaos doesn't pass down clear wins to the next generation, it spoils the soup.

/ / /

Watching Ada navigate sisterly love with Joanna, our wild little creature of a toddler, is a **wonder**⁶. I conspicuously wipe my eyes as she quietly passes on divine love through big-sister lessons. Like how to share the pink bunny. How to cover up with a blanket in bed. How to eat without spilling applesauce. How to stop demanding and demanding and demanding. How to navigate her beginner's Bible. It's her way of building up faith. She's "living out goodness, then adding to goodness knowledge, and to this divine knowledge a bit of self-control, and then perseverance in this big sister lifestyle of godliness, and to this godliness sisterly kindness, and finally on to kaleidoscopic love."[7] It's a wonder to witness.

Most evenings, Brooke and I sink into the couch with mixed drinks and cozy blankets astonished by these daily adventures in faith and deed. Small but divine moments wrapped in trials. Sure, some days we witness killjoy in full effect. But more often these adventures collide in the nexus of wisdom and imagination.

Parenting is a wild mystery. I think that's why awesome words and clear values are so vital beneath our roofs. They give us leverage in the chaos that bubbles up as we prepare a delicious soup. They push the villain back into the shadows while drawing out the living legend. There's a bit of wisdom tucked inside a better lexicon.

How's your soup brewing these days?

X

Xenia the Prince Warrior

I can still feel that stir in my gully I experienced on my first armchair adventure alongside Indiana Jones through the Temple of Doom. It was like an adult version of *The Goonies*, only with magic glowing rocks and a high-crown fedora. But it wasn't just the fedora that caught my attention, though mine still hangs in the closet. When the scene changed to that old church turned library, the mystery and myth of secret treasure grabbed my imagination. With buttery fingers I leaned forward as the III, VII and X etched before Jones' eyes became fulfilled beneath his feet.

X[1] always marks the spot.

It feels right to imagine mysterious destinations so clearly charted out. Some of us can smell the gold at the end of a treasure map on an uninhabited island. Or taste the salty sweat of victory at the end of a championship season with a promised trip to Disneyland. Others shift their eyes toward the glow of an "Adults Only" sign half a mile down the highway after a big sale. (Some Xs are more rewarding than others.)

Some of us are wired for extremes too. X is either the fullness of heaven set apart by God and the only thing worth tasting, or it's everything we can grasp, pillage and plunder in our search for X-ness. Yet, for most of us there's another, more obscure path in our wanderings.

Ever wonder what it felt like to experience that first night beyond the garden? "So the Lord God banished dirt-man from the garden of Eden to work the soil—the very soil he was drawn out of."[2] To experience the ultimate X and then lose your footing. To go from legend to lampoon in one foul bite of a sweetsop. Devastating? Sure, I get that, but what happened next? There's something in that gap worth tracing out. After all, no one is immune to losing out on an X at some point. We fumble the plan. We trample on the knowledge or the relationship or the opportunity. Some of us spit on the X pissed and bitter at the struggle. Some of us drop to our knees, stack stones and cry out until the tears run dry.

Imagine what Adam and Eve did that first night. Did they cower under a tree in fear of the wilds? Did they set out in search of another safe space? Did they gird up their loins without missing a beat, eager to plant their new garden away from *the* garden? I suppose it really doesn't matter what happened that first night or even that first week. What we see in the span of a sentence, post-banishment, is the shift from an outcast couple to a settled family with flocks and fields and a redeveloping relationship with Creator God. Turns out Garden X wasn't the end of the line for them.

I think our path is most often traveled somewhere down that track. Somewhere between bandera and brokenness. We tread the trail between selling all but our hiking sticks, and building new barns to store the overflow of our burgeoning greed. We navigate between joyfully relinquishing all, ready to grasp the treasure in Christ, and demanding more and more from others simply because they have what I lust for.

Adam and Eve rebuilt in the shadow of the garden. Moses led the masses toward a promised land full of milk and honey with a call for reentering into slavery. David was given a glimpse of the temple mount fully aware of how corrupting power can be. Each one teetered on the edge of divine X and doomsday, infused with the Spirit of God while embodying righteous purpose. Which leads me to believe that maybe our own tents and trials have something to offer this side of the ultimate X.

Years ago, after climbing out of the quintessential season of rejection, Brooke and I began to draft up images of life beyond the funk. We imagined white hair and slip-on shoes. Cozy chairs side by side on the front porch. Boisterous walks wild with grandkids. A deep faith washing over it all. Even now we'll walk around the house wondering how that old couple will connect the dots between these shoes and those slippers.

On the trail between extremes, my old American Foursquare marks the spot, yet it isn't really the house or the shoes or the slippers, is it? No matter how sturdy and peaceful and fulfilling this old place is, it's still a tent pitched in the shadow of garden hedges now grown high.

I think my home houses deeper things in the same way the ancient Tabernacle or Garden X did. It's a meeting ground for something more divine. A patch of dirt set apart for communion and fellowship. It's where I meet with my kids to impress on them God's divine way of life. Connect to share His covenant and experience His kingdom. Sit, walk and stand in pursuit of truth. Tell stories, share poems and sing spiritual songs. And tie symbols of faith and freedom around our hands and over our hearths.

But it's not about the mythical power of a golden chalice or a wooden cup or a hand-chiseled sandstone bowl. The utensils in a home, no matter how set apart for fostering a healthy family experience, are just utensils. The Holy Grail is about relationships.

"Rich, are you willing to worship Me? Drink this."

"R. J, are you willing to love Brooke with God's divine love? Take a sip."

"Dude, are you willing to guide your kids with the Spirit of truth and grace? Drink up." Sounds like more than an armchair adventure when you put it that way.

/ / /

It's a curious sort of sacrifice to open our door to a stranger made in God's image, isn't it? To open our home to God-breathed creatures down in the muck. Especially in those seasons when kids and husbands consume all the oxygen in every square inch of the home. How do neighbors and small groups and others find their way into these wild dens? This is where my lexicon has been steering lately.

Xenia[3] is an old Greek word for "hospitality." I like the sound of it too. Zen-ee-yah. Sort of makes me feel like a humble warrior prince opening his castle to the downtrodden. Pairs well with the marked spot above, doesn't it? A unique place of refreshment for those in need on their journeys. Like a rum and Coke pit stop on the front porch with a side of vanilla ice cream. Home away from home.

This princely hospitality is more than a garden hose for a thirsty dog. Xenia opens doors. It prepares extra food just in case. It has clean sheets and a spare room, or at least an inflatable mattress in the closet ready for a weary soul. This is such an awesome aspect of the Christian life. It puts the entire basket of spiritual fruit on full display right there in the foyer. And it's not about being the perfect host, either. Xenia might simply be a willing participant wading through a personal trial with a foggy idea about doing the right thing. Xenia might be exhausted, introverted, staving off a funk and yet willing.

Look, first of all, this is Christ's paradigm. Wrestle with Him if you have doubts.

Second, let's shift our perspective from fear to hope for a moment. Instead of attempting to quantify a potential houseguest's worthiness, what if we spend time discerning how to show the love of hospitality to this created creature? I'm guessing xenia is less about whether they deserve space under the roof of my X and more about my mindset in offering it.

From Jesus's perspective, it seems God is wildly interested in partnering with those of us who grasp this sort of sacrificial living. And from experience, we all seem to know of the omnidirectional ways Creator God moves to stir an aha here in the dirt: through the Word; through our world, both broken and beautiful; through prayer and that undeniable tug; through our kids' eyes and words; and yes, through strangers like ravens rapping on our doors.

Turns out, we aren't the first generation to press Him about this xenia lifestyle: "Lord, when did we see You hungry and feed You, or thirsty and give You something to drink? When did we see You a stranger and invite You in, or needing clothes and clothe You? When did we see You sick or in prison and go visit You?"[4]

"Listen closely," Jesus said, leaning in with a confident whisper, "whatever you did for the brothers or sisters of Mine in poverty, you did for Me."[5]

I think Jesus is inviting us onto that obscure middle path between eternal heaven and immediate indulgence. There's a divine experience standing on our welcome mat.

I'm not entirely naive. Being Xenia the prince warrior isn't just about opening up front doors and spare rooms and pantries. I have this amazing family inside—these unique creatures gifted to me and shaping my X to be the love and truth center I desire to live in. So if a creepy dude in a clown suit with a reputation for molesting kids and abusing hospitality for nefarious purposes needs a place to stay, my pull-out couch is probably going to be out of commission for the foreseeable future. Treasure is meant to be enjoyed, not raped, pillaged and plundered. I'd be glad to make a few calls, though.

Before Brooke entered my world, I opened my living room up to the wandering character freely—too freely. I spent many a late night with eyes open beneath the covers, waiting for the hatchet to burst through the door. This is why divine discernment plays a growing role in my lexicon. Discernment doesn't cancel out the movement of the Holy Spirit. No, it clarifies the wisdom to His work right here in my X.

But let's be honest, how many evil clowns do we come by on a daily basis? I've been there. Not behind the clown mask, but I've knocked on the door looking for a bed for my family. It's humbling to be on the other side of that threshold. It's worth a shift in perspective.

/ / /

I don't know about you, but even now it's easy for me to get caught up in the idea that the best Xs are out there on adventures alongside Indy. Caught up searching for treasure beyond the walls of my home, taunted by the sweet sounds of some other legendary mission. The truth is, though, more often than not, that so-called treasure is buried beneath a quagmire not worth mucking up life for.

At the end of the day, I'm sitting with my treasure right alongside Brooke and our band of wild curiosities. X is beneath our roof and within our guts, binding and loosing and breathing. After all, "Where our treasure is, that's where our xeniafied heart will be."[6]

How's that fedora feeling?

Y

Sexy You in YHWH

"You said in other countries it's dangerous to be a Christian, right?" Elias and I were talking politics.

"Some, yeah," I said.

"Illegal?"

"Converting to Christianity can be."

"How about in America?"

It's wild how an eleven-year-old's mind is curiously designed for big-picture politicking. When pejoratives and safe spaces and intersectionality are pushed aside, rational conversations, even with a kid, have room to breathe.

"Well, no, the founding fathers baked that freedom into the Constitution."

"Can it be dangerous?"

"What are you wondering about?"

"Just curious."

I liked the sound of that. "Hm. There's a group of representatives in one state who recently unanimously voted to condemn public expressions of faith which disagree with the ideological views of their small group of political leaders."

I watched the gears turn through his eyes. One eyebrow scrunched, and the other rose high. Rocking back and forth with pursed lips, he was processing at full capacity.

"Not a law. Just a show vote of their opinion, I guess. But there's always an act of individual persecution against one person or tribe or faith by another taking place in any given neighborhood."

The gears began to slow. "Dad, why don't they put themselves in the shoes of everyone else? I mean, how would they like it?"

In that one rational thought on grace within freedom, I watched Elias hike into manhood, LEGO bricks in one hand and a mighty pen in the other. Yes, he lacks chest hair, quietly rebuffs my invitation to watch zombie movies and can hardly see over the steering wheel, but he's fully aware of the harmful "me versus you" mindset. He understands that disagreement shouldn't be synonymous with danger or disdain.

This journey into a more engaging lexicon has cracked open the door to the closet stuffed with all the yous in my attitude. Cracked it open and pressed me to twist them inside out on the way to clarity. *You* are not the problem. *You* are not the one who needs to change. *You* are not the one living with a crappy attitude. You are not the one who should take the first step. You, Brooke, are not. You, Elias, are not. You, Ada, are not. You, Joanna…well, I think it's fair to say that you're a wild toddler in the throes of massive change and discovery. But no, you're not a thorn in my side either.

Politicking over coffee and donuts with my dude slapped an important missing brick into place. *You are not the source of all that ails me. I am the one wallowing in my own sin.*

When you're packed in a sweaty heap at a concert you bought tickets for three years prior and the lead singer gushes, "We're only here because of you!" it feels special, doesn't it? As though if Rich Dyson hadn't shown up, the show wouldn't have happened. In reality, though, *you* is plural, part of a mass of bodies.

But there's another you too. The unique **you**[1]. The man Brooke professes her love to while prepping homemade cinnamon rolls. A singular sentiment for my ears and my belly only.

I was thinking about this after Elias placed that block in my foundation. About how it would feel to ground my worldview a notch deeper in faith. Yeah, I know, those ancient, divinely-inspired letters were written *for* me, not *to* me. The authors wrote truths that benefit me even though I wasn't the original audience. I get it. But imagine if they had written with me in mind. What if John had autographed a letter for my eyes only? What if I was no longer a ticket in the crowd but a buddy to call after the show for a beer?

I imagine I would consume their letters with greater personal interest, right? I'd feel their intended heartbeat in each line. "I write these things to you who believe in the name of the Son of God so that you may know that you have eternal life."[2] A little stiff, I know, but John isn't one to waste words. Which is why his message hits at the core. "I'm writing this just for you, Rich. Do you understand?" Notice how John stresses you. He uses the word three times in this short passage, making it almost impossible for me to escape a personal confrontation with my faith.

John leaned in, pressed down firm on the paper and breathed these words with me in mind, as though he knew I'd need to hear this 2,000 years later. "Rich, I'm writing this to you, a future believer in the very Son of God I've personally seen and followed and believed in. I want you to know without a doubt that you have the eternal life Christ died for."

You.

Rich.

A unique individual who can believe the curious advent of your Creator with hope and discernment.

Rich, you can personally engage this God through your belief. Through a faith that is narrow and focused and pierces the soul.

/ / /

This perspective shifts things. Necessary things, like how I view my own worth. It's also a needed reminder of how much I want my kids to experience this reality. To witness their dad call each one of them by name, affirm their value here in the dirt and help them discover their personal skills, talents and banderas. This is why being intentional with our yous is so important. I get to endorse each of my kids' uniquely individual existence.

"You, Ada, are a co-creating princess in God's eternal kingdom." I get to say this while she squirms her way beneath that pink heart-speckled blanket at bedtime. I get to absorb her crazy smile and listen to one final random thought of the day. "You are cute and crazy and created to be right here. I love you. Good night."

"You, Elias, are wildly creative and willing and tenderhearted. You are."

"Joanna, you are quirky and quick-witted. You bring a grace-filled joy to every engagement."

But it's also important to call out the Dyson brood as a communal whole. We're part of something bigger here in the world. A world Christ deeply and sacrificially loves. My world.

"You, Dyson kids, are funtastically set apart to carry the Dyson name into the world with legendary curiosity and bold kindness. To model Christlikeness on this uniquely noble mission."

You has a lot of power, don't you think?

If we're not careful, our yous become nothing more than a half-hearted catch-all. Elias is not Ada is not Joanna. Different wiring, interests, gifts and personalities. And those one-on-one connects reveal their divine depth little by little.

One donut at a time.

One you at a time.

/ / /

I've been playing dress-up with Brooke lately. (No, not that kind. Her shoes are too tight.) I've been trying to view our little world through her lens. Mostly, I want to spy on my own words and actions and decisions from around the corner to find the biases lurking and loafing. You know, some of those condescending views secretly shaping my vision of the world around me. Hidden thoughts generally draped over an audience because of a rotten experience at the gas station. Self-deprecating judgment of my parenting style because of an article I read three years ago in a different season of life, by someone with different values in a different context.

But I also want to find growth. I want to find the strengths building after a limited lifetime of study and experience. I want to encourage that bald man to keep going because, after all, how else am I going to fill into my *imago Dei*? I want to pretend to be Brooke peering in on her amazingly well-adjusted hubby to catch a better look for a better day.

"Super sexy the way your monosyllabic yes has become a heartfelt response."

"Oh, baby! The way you're beginning to weigh your understanding through the lens of my point of view? Mm-hmm!"

"Nothing more attractive than your tender voice getting the kids ready for bed."

Suburban sexy. Maybe it's not so difficult to saunter around in her shoes.

Peeking in on that super-sexy gardener, I've noticed a man with a refreshed desire to understand the I AM behind these "you are" revelations.

Remember when Moses first encountered Creator God in the desert, barefoot and terrified? He had no concrete beliefs about this divine Bush-Being. Yet in one unique interaction, he discerned that this ancient God calling out to him from a fiery plant—a God who simply referred to Himself as the Eternal Existence, **YHVH**[3], the I AM and WILL BE—was more personal than any Egyptian idol from his past.

"Moses, take a breath, remove your sandals and call me YHVH."[4]

That brushfire talkin' to me? Okay. Don't black out, Mo. Remove sandals. Bend the knees.

"Moses, you are called, filled and empowered. Now go to them and say, 'You need to listen to I AM.'"[5]

My heart's gonna explode! Just breathe, man. You cannot pass out in front of God.

Can you imagine the divine tension between "you" and I AM? Here's Moses, a runaway, nomadic sheep keeper, confronting the Eternal Existence face to burning face. Moses is singled out by God. The message and the mission are personalized. "Moses. *I* will be with *you*."

Look, I'm aware that I'm not Moses. Not even *like* Moses. Yet we're united in this strange nexus of revelation. Moses, spying on his flock across the wilds with sandals and staff, had a keen sense of his surroundings that alerted him to an untended fire. Rich, spying on himself across the room with tight shoes and cane, has a growing awareness of something divine in the works. At the nexus of these observations, a holy YHVH, several-thousand-years apart, reaches out with a personal invitation to a personal relationship with Him, which spills over onto others.

And like a multi-layered story, Rabbi Jesus shows up, somewhere between Moses and Rich, with the same invitation as YHVH into the same way of being alongside the same God. "I am the way, the truth and the life. You will not reach the Father of the Burning Bush without first trusting in Me. I AM the way. I AM the truth. I AM the life. I AM the nexus. I AM and I WILL BE with you, Rich. Now take off those tight shoes and follow Me."[6]

This is precisely the moment when standing in Brooke's shoes isn't necessary anymore. It's when my focus tangibly shifts from self-righteousness or self-deprecation to YHVH. When my life rhythm moves from the quagmire of "me versus you" into the river of "you and I are sexy beings made in the image of the I AM."

/ / /

Turns out, Elias was right. You aren't the problem. I just needed to slip into another's shoes for a season. Yeah, those sociopolitical shoes are important for sure. But swapping shoes with my partner, my friend, my wife? Putting on Brooke's strengths and walking alongside myself? Stepping into her anxieties and sharing a meal and a bed with me? Now that offers omnidimensional insight far beyond even the most culturally sensitive shoes. Why? Because she's in the best position to show me who I really am when no one's looking. Which makes it tempting to put on my Captain Killjoy hat. At the sight of my weaknesses, I'm inclined to sink into an old quagmire and sabotage the potential aha. But I'm tired of losing her shoes in the mud.

At the end of the day, you and I are just a couple of awkward, bandera-waving, melancholic legends wearing our wives' shoes in the backyard, teary-eyed as YHVH calls out, "You! You are made on purpose. You are forgiven for all that muck-flinging. You are because I AM. Now lay down those rocks and follow Me." It's a curious shift, isn't it?

Thank God He's breaking down these old walls and shields and "you are" -isms. How about you? Have you discovered just how valuable you are in the burning light of YHVH? Maybe, just maybe, you need to take a good look at your sexy self long enough to realize that it's not really about you.

Whose shoes are you wearing lately?

Z

Zenith of Zeal

A few summers back, at that seminar on healing emotional wounds, an aha snuck in through the cracks. Late one morning, from the main stage, we were challenged to find a quiet space, settle in and listen for God. Though I'd registered with this sort of practice in mind, my innate rebellion rolled its eyes at the mandate. *Force my beating heart to pause as though Creator God will arrive simply because it's on the itinerary? And right before lunch!* Thankfully curiosity didn't kill this cat and I wound up sitting beneath the June sun in a paved lot on the sidewalk. I sat there like a toddler, awkwardly trying not to fidget in my quiet space, listening.

Listening for God in nature.

Listening for God to speak through His Word.

Listening for God's voice deep within my gut.

It sort of felt like forcing an X to be the spot just because I wanted it to be there. It felt impossible.

The sharp hum of a flatlining monitor rang in my ears, audible residue from my former life as a musician without earplugs. Cars slipped by with wide-eyed drivers wearing small-toothed grins, shrugging as they passed. I watched them follow their stomachs for a while, but eventually,

I closed my eyes, counted my breaths and slid out of my sandals. Then, abruptly, I was no longer simply perched on the front walk of a megachurch, I was transported to a garden. And I was helplessly aware of His advent.

The breeze moved in with a **zealous**[1] whisper: "Rich, are you listening?"

I could hear it gather steam across the lot. "Rich, it's time to look up once and for all."

Rising it rushed through the empty sky, "Stand up, man! Move forward. Speak forward. Live forward!"

Like an excited child searching for the right words, the wind dashed in all directions until it at last burst my personal bubble. With goose-bumps now rolling across my arms like waves, this wild breeze rummaged through pockets and swirled down my favorite button-up. As it passed it filled my throat with the warm blacktop air. I couldn't utter a sound.

My eyes opened toward the treetops beyond the lot. Their giant limbs waved like stalks of grain silently swaying to an old Dylan song. And then, suffocating silence. It seemed the Creator had stepped down, captured my attention, then rushed on to refresh another desperately distracted soul.

It was startling just how little control I had over my spiritual faculties. I set the stage, of course—removing headphones, silencing the ringer, setting aside my journals and flicking away all encroaching pebbles— yet even still, in those pre-lunch twenty minutes, I wasn't quite invested. I couldn't seem to clear the noise in my mind or force a peep from Creator God.

But that's precisely when He arrived at my paved altar, casting off the villainous killjoy with nothing more than a breeze and whisper.

Remember when Jesus said, "Take heart! I've overcome the world"?[2]

Well, soon after shouting that bold proclamation He really did overcome the world. He beat the lost zealots at their own game. He rose from death. And before stepping from dust to throne, He said to you and to me, "Listen, I will absolutely be with you always, to the very end of the age."[3] Catch that? Those of us who feel and hear and see and believe in His breathed-out Word, we're gifted an eternal traveling mate.

Even now, right here on my front porch at the other end of the journey, I can feel that breeze, hear that whisper and taste the blacktop of that serendipitous aha. A God zealous to share His love. A Creator eager to know and be known. A Salvager in pursuit of souls to reclaim and refresh. It makes sense that in His zeal He would take me up on my half-hearted offer to listen. It's what parents do, right? We patiently wait for opportunities to breathe wisdom and refreshment into the lives of our kids. No, they're not always eager to receive it, but we're ready to fill their hearts and minds regardless. If only in passing. I can imagine how the disciples felt after every meal with the Messiah.

/ / /

If you'd asked me before this journey toward a better lexicon, I'd have pushed back on the role of zeal. The word has always been a bit of a turnoff. It brings to mind the picture of a religious zealot in a tunic with daggers and conspiracies. A political snake with poisoned agenda zealously trampling and tromping his way to power.

You've seen him slither in with a shiv only to hear, "Et tu, Brute?"

Or kiss the cheek before, "Friend, do what you came for."[4]

I know, I've robbed zeal of its divine light. I've plunged it into the blackened heart of a killjoy on doomsday who shouts, "God bless the queen!" But it's fair to say that zeal in a wounded and deceived heart often leads to the pain and suffering of others, isn't it? Crucifixion ring a bell? "Father, forgive them. In their misdirected zeal they don't know what they're doing."[5]

On the other hand, zeal, birthed in the ashes of a doomsday and eager to forgive and flourish, is actually sourced in something greater. Someone uniquely noble. The very same crucifixion churned up by those rabid zealots? Yeah, divine zeal emanates from there.

And this zeal isn't bitter and busted-up like some insecure heartthrob. No, it's filled to the brim with a kaleidoscopic **zest**[6] for life. The same refreshment I began searching for in the ashes of my own burned bridges years ago.

/ / /

Back on my porch I've been reading Paul's letter to those ancient Ephesian believers. It's personal, again. "I pray also that the eyes of your heart, Rich, may be enlightened in order that you may know the hope to which he has called you, the riches of his inheritance in the saints and his incomparably great power for us who believe."[7] Imagine waking up to this reality each and every day. Like fresh-squeezed orange juice and super crispy bacon in bed. Christ's hope and inheritance and power consumed by the innermost parts of our being at the start of each day.

Eyes consume things, right? Sure, we have different appetites and diets, but consumption works the same.

"Would you like a slice of cheesecake?" I can taste it across the room.

"I'll pay in cash." Love me some leafy greens.

"Looks like everyone's at the beach today." It's called eye candy for a reason, right?

It's an endless barrage of unsatisfying laxatives. We eat them whole and turn back for more. We roam and consume and choke, stuck in the quagmire of lust, sloshing around in our own drool. And then we sprint to the bathroom.

I think that's why Paul's prayer is so dynamic. It's about experiencing the **zeniths**[8] as they are, moments of divine refreshment set apart for a legacy of purpose in pursuit of a bandera that matters. If we're not careful, the eyes of our heart will swallow up everything in their path. And the lexicon overflowing from such a perverted heart isn't interested in listening for God in the wind. It's not interested in healthy community or personal responsibility or true freedom. It's too busy filling its stomach.

These zeniths carry an old magic, don't they? C.S. Lewis used to write about this deep magic. I think it's the same sort that opened the eyes of my heart, starving for a better lexicon. And it isn't that this divine lexicon has wiped out the melancholy, though God knows I've asked. Rather, the divine melody woven throughout my growing lexicon hums along in the nexus of sweetened highs and mellowed lows.

Magic does that sort of thing. Like baptism—not the water so much as the Spirit's washing off the muck and sucking out the poison. Of course some thorns and logs remain, but maybe it's to goad us on toward the source of all magic. The source of better words and ideas and lives. Whether by magic or by thorn, my growing lexicon seems to foster more and more life each and every day.

No doubt I'm able to live a new lexicon because Christ lived it first. All of it. And the God that stirred my heart to call out, "Ada, you're awesome!" on those monkey bars is the same Redeemer who stepped into that parking lot to whisper, "Rich, you're awesome too."

Words are often His mode of choice. Songs, whispers, guttural yawps. "In the beginning was the Word"[9] and that Word, along with all words worth shouting to the heavens from my front porch, have been set apart for my divine journey. For my marriage. For my home. For the others I don't yet understand. It's amazing what words can build in the mouth of a humble wordsmith.

And these words are set apart for you too.

You already have some. We all do. A handful of words to describe that handful of divinely orchestrated heaven-on-earth experiences. Moments that reach the peak of all things spirit and flesh. A zesty pulp of faith and deed. Struggle and salvage. Wind and the whispers.

How's your lexicon shaping up these days? My own lexiconical adventure isn't nearly over. I'm a newer man, without a doubt, yet there are quite a few elusive words out there under rocks and between ribs waiting to pounce on my heart and tongue. Can you hear the words out there waiting for you? They move like wind and sound like hope. They crash like waves and carry like true love. I suppose we can't schedule these discoveries with Creator God, but we can expect them.

Are you listening?

May God enlighten you at the advent of your journey toward that bandera of dreams. May He comfort you in the muck of momentary lapses in judgment. May you remember to pause, listen for the sound of His Spirit on the path ahead and stand firm as the priest or priestess of Christ in your home. May you and I grasp the height and depth of our call to love God, love others and love ourselves right here in the dirt. May your divine lexicon spill over like fresh paint on the awesome canvas of your life.

REFLECT
Now What?

Well, self-reflection is a divinely human trait. Ask yourself a few questions. What's God showing you? What are you learning about how Christ has wired you? How are you going to respond?

Q. Are you breathing out the words you imagine building a strong, healthy and hope-filled home with?

Q. Which three words / phrases do you use that you know disrupt, destroy and divide your divine journey and the adventures of those closest to you? Write them down.

Q. Each phrase you wrote down is toxic. Now, what three words / phrases, born out of the ancient Biblical truth of faith, hope and love, will you counter your own despair with? Write these down.

Q. So, which elemental values are you grasping tightly to on a daily basis? And which have you been missing out on for too long?

Q. Others will attempt to define you, your bandera and your rhythm of life. How are you allowing God's Word to define you as a valuable parent, entrepreneur, servant and faithful worshipper with a vision?

Q. Mindset impacts every nook and cranny of our lives. How does your internal dialogue shape your external rhythm of life and language?

Q. Every struggle, wound and failure is an opportunity for growth, insight and redemption. How is Jesus shaping your attitude? Are you building up or tearing down?

Endnotes

████

A

1 Awesome: extraordinary, terrific; inspiring and/or expressing awe

2 Advent: coming into being, or use

3 Aha: an expression of surprise or triumph

4 Deut. 31:6, author's paraphrase

5 Ada: adornment; ornament; beautiful addition; first daughter

6 Matt. 5:14–16, author's paraphrase

B

1 Bandera: flag, pennant; colors - www.lexico.com

2 John 14:6, author's paraphrase

3 Birth: the act or process of bringing forth; the emergence; to be born

4 Brooke: creek; tolerate—Brooke lives up to this definition in that her voice is like the plentiful and sweet sound of a river. But also that she tolerates my ways.

5 Bottleneck: narrow route; point of congestion; to slow or halt the flow

C

1 Can: be able to; a possibility

2 2 Cor. 5:7, author's paraphrase

3 2 Eph. 1:19, author's paraphrase

4 Creator: one that creates, usually by bringing something new or original into being—You and I are made by The Creator. We're created co-creators.

5 Curious: an eagerness to learn and gain knowledge. Inquisitive in nature. Strange and unusual.

6 Gen. 2:24

D

1 Discernment: to grasp and comprehend; the ability and act of perceiving

2 Phil. 2:1–3, author's paraphrase

3 Phil. 1:9-10

4 Doomsday: a day of catastrophic destruction; final judgment

5 Diligence: steady, earnest, energetic effort; perseverance

6 Heb. 11:33

7 vv. 35-36

8 v. 34

E

1 Endless: being or seeming to be without end

2 Element: weather conditions; an essential part

3 Encourage: to inspire with courage, spirit or hope; to spur onward

4 John 14:15-20, author's paraphrase

5 Elias: YHVH is God, a variant of Elijah

F

1 amusement; mockery; a violent argument

2 Freedom: the absence of constraint in choice or action

3 Gal. 5:1, author's paraphrase

4 Fantastic: fantasy, seemingly conceived by unrestrained fancy; exceedingly great; eccentric

5 Future: what is to come; occurring at a later time; an expectation of advancement

G

1 Good: of a favorable character or tendency; virtuous, right, commendable

2 Luke 18:19, author's paraphrase

3 Grace: unmerited divine favor or assistance from God; disposition to or an act or instance of kindness; state of sanctification

4 Gift: to endow with; to present with; given willingly without payment

H

1 How: in what manner, method or way

2 Psa. 25:9

3 Humility: freedom from pride or arrogance; the quality or state of being humble

4 Humble: not proud; reflecting, expressing, or offered in a spirit of deference or submission

5 Eph. 5:21

6 v. 25, author's paraphrase

7 vv. 26–27, author's paraphrase

8 Hurt: to inflict with physical pain; to cause emotional pain or anguish; to wrong; to suffer

9 Hope: to desire with expectation of future fulfillment; to trust that God is engaged in our good and for His glory

10 Phil. 1:6, author's paraphrase

I

1 Invest: to make use of for future benefits or advantages; to endow with a quality; to cover

2 Exod. 3:11, author's paraphrase

3 Neh. 2:5

4 Interest: something or someone that arouses attention; to engage, induce or persuade to interest

5 Matt. 22:37, 39, author's paraphrase

6 Imagine: to form a mental image of something not present; to believe

7 Matt. 25:21

J

1 Joanna: named in honor of my mom, Joann, with the added 'a' for Brooke's pleasure. Joanna is a feminine form of John—God is gracious.

2 Psa. 47:1, author's paraphrase

3 Joy: a source of delight; a state of happiness, experiencing great pleasure

4 Col. 3:16, author's paraphrase

5 Jump: move energetically; to show eagerness; to move haphazardly or irregularly

6 Luke 14:28-30

K

1 Kind: sympathetic or helpful nature, gentle, to give pleasure or relief; a state of being

2 Gal. 5:22–23

3 Tit. 3:4–5

4 Matt. 18:20

5 Killjoy: one who spoils the pleasures of others

6 Kaleidoscope: a continually changing pattern of shapes and colors

L

1 Lampoon: a harsh satire (witty sarcasm used to mock or expose folly) directed against someone; the subject of a lampoon

2 Legend: a popular myth; a body of stories; a person or thing that inspires stories and tales

3 Legacy: something transmitted from a predecessor or from the past

4 1 John 4:8

5 John 10:30

6 John 14:20

7 Love: n. strong affection; v. to hold dear; 1 John 4:7-16, love is translated from the Greek agapē & agapaō: to love, esteem, cherish

8 1 John 3:16, author's paraphrase

M

1 Mindset: a mental attitude or inclination; a fixed state of mind

2 Phil. 2:5, NLT

3 Attitude: a mental position with regard to fact or state; a bodily state of readiness to respond in a characteristic way

4 Luke 23:34

5 Message: a messengers mission; a communication in writing, speech or by signals

6 Mission: a specific task a person or group is charged with; a self-imposed objective or purpose

N

1 No: used to express negation, dissent, denial, or refusal; to express the negative or an alternative choice or possibility

2 Eph. 2:10, author's paraphrase

3 Matt. 6:24

4 Nexus: connection, link; a connected group

O

1 Others: adj. being the one or ones distinct from those first implied; n. a different or additional one

2 Gen. 12:1–2, author's paraphrase

3 John 8:7, author's paraphrase

4 Omnidimensional: in all angles, directions and dimensions (of life and time and space and faith)

5 Eph. 3:14–19, author's paraphrase

6 Onymous: bearing a name

7 Exod. 3:13–14, author's paraphrase

P

1 Purpose: intent, something set up as an object or end to be obtained

2 Matt. 22:37–39, author's paraphrase

3 1 John 1:5

4 Pissed: angry, irritated, annoyed

5 Perspective: a mental view; our capacity to view things in their true relations or relative importance

6 Matt. 13:16, author's paraphrase

Q

1 Quintessential: representative; an element that is a typical part or pure example

2 Question: an interrogative expression often used to test knowledge; asking; doubt or objection

3 Quagmire: trapped, a precarious situation

4 Matt. 28:20, author's paraphrase

5 Gal. 2:20, author's paraphrase

6 John 17:21-23, author's paraphrase

R

1 Righteous: acting according to divine or moral law

2 Gen. 15:6

3 Rebellion: opposition to one in authority or power

4 Reliable: yielding the same results in succession; dependable

5 Raise: to set upright by lifting or building; to stir up, awaken; to cultivate, bring to maturity

6 Raze: destroy to the ground; scrape, cut or shave off

7 Psa. 121:1–4, 8, author's paraphrase

S

1 Psa. 23:1-3, 6

2 Serendipity: the phenomenon of finding valuable or agreeable things not sought for—Sure, these serendipitous events may very well be providence.

3 Serve: to be useful, to help; to be reliable

4 John 9:1-11

5 Luke 13:10-13

6 Salvage: to rescue or save especially from wreckage or ruin

7 Savior: deliverer, preserver | (Hebrew) yeshuwah: salvation, deliverance

8 Psa. 23:5

T

1 Matt. 22:37, author's paraphrase

2 v. 39, author's paraphrase

3 1 Cor. 12:31, author's paraphrase

4 1 John 4:8

5 Trial: a test of faith, patience or stamina through subjection, suffering or temptation

6 Jas. 1:2–4, author's paraphrase

7 Test: a basis for evaluation

8 Rom. 5:3–4

9 Terrify: to drive or impel by menacing; Terror: a state of intense or overwhelming fear

10 Phil. 2:17

11 Thankful: conscious of benefit received; well pleased

12 Rom. 12:1

U

1 Union: the joining or uniting two or more things into one; something that is made one

2 Heb. 1:2-3a

3 Unique: the only one, distinct, without like or equal

4 Useless: having or being of no use; unable to serve

5 Philem. v. 11, author's paraphrase

6 Philem. v. 20, author's paraphrase

V

1 John 15:2, author's paraphrase

2 Value: an important principle or preference with intrinsic value, quality or worth

3 Jas. 4:1–2, author's paraphrase

4 Villain: scoundrel; one blamed for a particular evil or difficulty

5 Gal. 5:19-20

6 John 16:33, author's paraphrase

W

1 Wisdom: the ability to discern qualities and relationships; wise attitude, belief or course of action

2 Author's paraphrase

3 Matt. 19:21, 26:26–27, 8:20, 16:24, 28:20, author's paraphrase

4 Matt. 16:24 & Luke 23:39-43, author's paraphrase

5 Wild: passionately eager or enthusiastic; going beyond normal or conventional bounds; strong passion, emotion or desire; wild, free or natural state of existence; off the intended course

6 Wonder: a cause of astonishment or admiration; to feel surprise; to feel curiosity

7 2 Pet. 1:5–7, author's paraphrase

X

1 X: an idiom for a target or exact location

2 Gen. 3:23, author's paraphrase

3 Xenia: Greek adj. hospitality; n. place of lodging and rest

4 Matt. 25:37-49

5 v. 40, author's paraphrase

6 Matt. 6:21, author's paraphrase

Y

1 You: the one or ones being addressed

2 1 John 5:13

3 YHVH: I Am; LORD; tetragrammaton—the four-letter Hebrew word for God, often articulated as Yahweh

4 Exod. 3:5–6, author's paraphrase

5 v. 12, 14, author's paraphrase

6 John 14:6-7, author's paraphrase

Z

1 Zealous: adj. marked by fervent partisanship for a person, a cause, or an ideal; zeal: n. eagerness and ardent interest in the pursuit of something

2 John 16:33

3 Matt. 28:20, author's paraphrase

4 Matt. 26:50, author's paraphrase

5 Luke 23:34, author's paraphrase

6 Zest: an enjoyable, exciting quality; a feeling of enjoyment or enthusiasm

7 Eph. 1:18–19, author's paraphrase

8 Zenith: culminating point; the highest point reached in the heavens by man

9 John 1:1

LE XI CO N of Ā WE SO ME